Nº 5 PLATFORM

GREAT EASTERN RAILWAY
PETERBOROUGH and G.N. MIDLAND and
L & N.W. RAILWAYS
SPALDING and LINCOLN
GAINSBOROUGH and DONCASTER
ALL STATIONS to LINCOLN and DONCASTER
via CAMBRIDGE and LONDON
CHATTERIS ST. IVES and CAMBRIDGE
WISBECH LYNN HUNSTANTON
and
PETERBORO Local Trains

The
GOLDEN AGE
of the
RAILWAY POSTER

The GOLDEN AGE of the RAILWAY POSTER

J T Shackleton

CHARTWELL BOOKS INC.

The GOLDEN AGE of the RAILWAY POSTER

Published by Chartwell Books Inc., A Division of Book Sales Inc., 110 Enterprise Avenue, Secaucus, New Jersey 07094

Text copyright © JT Shackleton 1976

Illustrations copyright © New English Library 1976

Designed by Roger Judd

Set in Old Style by South Bucks Typesetters Ltd, 26A Aylesbury End, Beaconsfield, Bucks.

First published in Great Britain by New English Library, Barnard's Inn, Holborn, London EC1N 2JR in 1976.

ISBN O-89009-121-8

PRINTED IN ITALY

Front endpaper: Fort William station, West Highland Railway, around the turn of the century, with displays of pictorial and typographical posters on the walls. *WS Sellar collection*

Rear endpaper: March station on the Great Eastern Railway in 1905. Railway posters are much in evidence on the island platform buildings. *Arnold Wood collection*

CONTENTS

THE
STOCKTON & DARLINGTON
RAILWAY COMPANY
Hereby give Notice,

THAT the FORMAL OPENING of their RAILWAY will take place on the 27th instant, as announced in the public Papers.—The Proprietors will assemble at the Permanent Steam Engine, situated below BRUSSELTON TOWER*, about nine Miles West of DARLINGTON, at 8 o'clock, and, after examining their extensive inclined Planes there, will start from the Foot of the BRUSSELTON descending Plane, at 9 o'clock, in the following Order :——

1. THE COMPANY'S LOCOMOTIVE ENGINE.
2. The ENGINE'S TENDER, with Water and Coals.
3. SIX WAGGONS, laden with Coals, Merchandize, &c.
4. The COMMITTEE, and other PROPRIETORS, in the COACH belonging to the COMPANY.
5. SIX WAGGONS, with Seats reserved for STRANGERS.
6. FOURTEEN WAGGONS, for the Conveyance of Workmen and others.

☞ The WHOLE of the above to proceed to STOCKTON.

7. SIX WAGGONS, laden with Coals, to leave the Procession at the DARLINGTON BRANCH.
8. SIX WAGGONS, drawn by Horses, for Workmen and others.
9. Ditto   Ditto.
10. Ditto   Ditto.
11. Ditto   Ditto.

The COMPANY'S WORKMEN to leave the Procession at DARLINGTON, and DINE at that Place at ONE o'clock; excepting those to whom Tickets are specially given for YARM, and for whom Conveyances will be provided, on their Arrival at STOCKTON.

TICKETS will be given to the Workmen who are to dine at DARLINGTON, specifying the Houses of Entertainment.

The PROPRIETORS, and such of the NOBILITY and GENTRY as may honour them with their Company, will DINE precisely at THREE o'clock, at the TOWN-HALL, STOCKTON.— Such of the Party as may incline to return to DARLINGTON that Evening, will find Conveyances in waiting for their Accommodation, to start from the COMPANY'S WHARF there precisely at SEVEN o'clock.

The COMPANY take this Opportunity of enjoining on all their WORK-PEOPLE that Attention to *Sobriety* and *Decorum* which they have hitherto had the Pleasure of observing.

The COMMITTEE give this PUBLIC NOTICE, that all Persons who shall ride upon, or by the sides of, the RAILWAY, on Horseback, will incur the Penalties imposed by the Acts of Parliament passed relative to this RAILWAY.

* Any Individuals desirous of seeing the Train of Waggons descending the inclined Plane from ETHERLEY, and in Progress to BRUSSELTON, may have an Opportunity of so doing, by being on the RAILWAY at ST. HELEN'S AUCKLAND not later than Half-past Seven o'clock.

RAILWAY-OFFICE, *Sept. 19th,* 1825.

ATKINSON's Office, High-Row, Darlington.

1 Printed handbill advertising the opening of the Stockton and Darlington Railway, 27 September 1825. Like the Surrey Iron Railway toll-sheet, the design of this bill owes more to eighteenth century broadsides and proclamations than to advertisements proper.
Durham County Library

2 A useful method of taking posters outside the normal railway sites and into the streets was to affix them to the delivery vans and buses operated by many railways. For many years the Great Western Railway also operated buses bedecked with posters which toured the country advertising railway services.
Great Western Railway Museum, Swindon

Introduction

Railways are many-faceted undertakings, and over the years the variety of subjects which they present has attracted the attention of countless chroniclers. Locomotive technicalities, profiles of engineers and designers, the histories of particular lines – all have received their fair share of historical coverage. Yet, curiously, comparatively scant attention seems to have been paid by the specialist railway historians to what, in the eyes of the travelling public, might seem to be one of the most immediate aspects of railways, namely their public face. Of the architecture and design of railway premises, thanks to the efforts of such writers as Gordon Biddle, Sir Nikolaus Pevsner and Sir John Betjeman, we know a fair amount but, in view of the amount of material still physically available, still not nearly enough. A good deal has been published about the workings of passenger trains in the Victorian era, but there is surprisingly little information about the interior decorations and fittings of the carriages. Brian Haresnape has made some extremely valuable studies of industrial design as applied to railways, but perhaps the most neglected field of all in terms of the relative scale of effect which it has had on those using railways, has been that of poster advertising. This book is intended as an introductory coverage of this most important area.

For advertising, quite apart from its value to the art historian or to the nostalgic, can tell us much about railway companies which may not be outwardly obvious from a study of the more technically oriented aspects which are the usual subjects of railway histories: the pride a company felt in its services,

2

the image which it felt itself to have (or wished upon itself), the type of traffic it was anxious to capture. The images which it chose to present to the travelling public may not have been a true reflection of its reality; most people, asked to define what a railway means to them, would speak in terms of draughty stations, stale sandwiches and trains which always run late. In poster advertising, we are offered an opportunity to fantasise and to escape from all this, into a world of gay holiday travel, luxurious dining cars and hotels and fast, efficient services. This world immediately excites the imagination; it is, of course, commercially intended to do so and to lure us on to the trains as a result.

Through the work of the 'hidden persuader' we can, too, see a little of the changing patterns of our recent social history, from the novelty and excite-

ment of early excursion travel through the rumbustuous era of the seaside holiday to the chic period of international travel. I make no pretence that this account is definitive; posters are by nature ephemeral, and there are no doubt many memorable designs which have long since crumbled to dust or been lost under the accrued lumber of the years. It has also been disconcerting to find how little official documentation of railway advertising has survived the passage of time. With what remains, though, I have attempted to convey the general patterns of the subject over the past century or so, to show what was typical as well as to show what was exceptional. And I hope that some of the qualities of splendour, charm, humour, naivety, outrage and sheer delightfulness which I have found in these relics of a bygone age will communicate themselves to the reader.

I would like to express my thanks, firstly to the numerous authorities and private collectors (notably Victor Goldberg, Derek Brough and M. Pierre Delacroix and his staff at *La Vie du Rail* in Paris) who have permitted me access to their material, provided information and pointed out further avenues of research, and also to Alice Shackleton, Geoff Hemstedt, Ian and Lucy Krause, Paul Siebel, Richard Evans, Gram and Emmylou, Janet Sacks and others who, in one way and another, kept me reasonably sane and on the right track.

J. T. Shackleton
London
November 1975

3 Pages from the July 1913 issue of the *Railway and Travel Monthly*, a forerunner of the present *Railway Magazine*. This periodical had occasional features on current railway posters, and the excellent colour reproductions and commentary are a useful source of material from this period. In the top left-hand poster one can see the English language version of Fig 85.
Derek Brough collection (Ian Krause)

---

4 A more overtly commercial bill from the Stockton and Darlington, embodying the use of fat face display letters, decorated rule, reversed panel and other devices calculated to arrest the attention. Similar notices could be found advertising stage coach and shipping services at the same period. The *Experiment* coach itself was little more than a conventional stage coach fitted with rail wheels.
British Rail

Chapter One

Anticipations of the Railway Poster

Railways and printing existed independently of each other for nearly four centuries, largely because the earliest railways were not public commercial undertakings and thus had no need to avail themselves of advertisements (a very early use of printing) to make their presence felt. Until the beginning of the nineteenth century, railways were private affairs used, for instance, for the carriage of coal from colliery to loading point. By that time, in other sectors of the commercial world, advertising was in full swing, in newspapers, in the form of posters on walls, and as handbills distributed amongst the population.

It was only when railways began to offer their services to the general public that they instituted the distribution of promotional handbills and posters to make their facilities compete with the alternative services offered by road and water-borne transport. The world's first public railway was the Surrey Iron Railway, authorised by Act of Parliament in 1801. It ran from the dock basin at Wandsworth, south of the Thames, to Croydon in Surrey. In form (for this was still many years before the application of steam power to railway locomotion became an economic possibility) it was little different from the many other waggonways in other parts of the country; the horse was the staple of motive power, the waggons (known as chaldrons, an archaic term still in use in the north-east until very recent years) had stout wooden bodies and iron flangeless wheels, and the track was angled into an L-shape for guidance and carried on stone block sleepers. Some of these sleepers can still be seen in the eastern wall of the present Young's

brewery near the Wandsworth basin. What made the Surrey Iron Railway unique, and thus caused them to produce their printed bill of June 1804, was the fact that anyone could bring along his horse and cart (providing, of course, that the wheels were the correct distance apart) and run it along the course of the railway, upon payment of the tolls indicated.

Despite the decorated rule being carelessly off-centre, this toll-sheet was an attractive example of the neatness and airiness of design which characterised eighteenth-century bills and broadsheets and which was carried through into the early years of the nineteenth century, until Thorne's full-face letters, introduced in 1803, rapidly became the standard for display advertising. It would seem, though, that it is now the only surviving example of a notice from the very earliest public railways. Though there were a number of these in the early years of the nineteenth century, notably the Canterbury and Whitstable Railway (the first to use steam locomotives for regular passenger services in 1830), the Oystermouth Railway (later the Swansea and Mumbles and in 1804, the very first to carry passengers at all) and the Middleton Railway (still working today), nothing in the way of toll-sheets or printed regulations from these seems to be in existence today.

The beginnings of railway advertising proper can be said to have coincided with the opening of the Stockton and Darlington Railway on Tuesday, 27 September 1825. The line was engineered by George Stephenson, and in view of his close association with the development of steam locomotives on

SURREY
Iron Railway.

The COMMITTEE of the SURREY IRON RAILWAY COMPANY,

HEREBY, GIVE NOTICE,. That the BASON at *Wandsworth*, and the Railway therefrom up to *Croydon* and *Carfhalton*, is now open for the Ufe of the Public, on Payment of the following Tolls, *viz.*

For all Coals entering into or going out of their Bason at Wandsworth,	*per Chaldron,*	3d.
For all other Goods entering into or going out of their Bason at Wandsworth - -	*per Ton,*	3d.

For all GOODS carried on the said RAILWAY, as follows, viz.

For Dung, - -	*per Ton, per Mile,*	1d.
For Lime, and all Manures, (except Dung,) Lime-ftone, Chalk, Clay, Breeze, Afhes, Sand, Bricks, Stone, Flints, and Fuller's Earth,	*per Ton, per Mile,*	2d.
For Coals, - -	*per Chald. per Mile,*	3d.
And, For all other Goods, -	*per Ton, per Mile,*	3d.

By ORDER of the COMMITTEE,

W. B. LUTTLY,

Wandsworth, June 1, 1804.

Clerk of the Company.

BROOKE, PRINTER, No. 35, PATERNOSTER-ROW, LONDON.

1829.

GRAND COMPETITION

OF

LOCOMOTIVES

ON THE

LIVERPOOL & MANCHESTER RAILWAY.

STIPULATIONS & CONDITIONS

ON WHICH THE DIRECTORS OF THE LIVERPOOL AND MANCHESTER RAILWAY OFFER A PREMIUM OF £500 FOR THE MOST IMPROVED LOCOMOTIVE ENGINE.

I.

The said Engine must "effectually consume its own smoke," according to the provisions of the Railway Act, 7th Geo. IV.

II.

The Engine, if it weighs Six Tons, must be capable of drawing after it, day by day, on a well-constructed Railway, on a level plane, a Train of Carriages of the gross weight of Twenty Tons, including the Tender and Water Tank, at the rate of Ten Miles per Hour, with a pressure of steam in the boiler not exceeding Fifty Pounds on the square inch.

III.

There must be Two Safety Valves, one of which must be completely out of the reach or control of the Engine-man, and neither of which must be fastened down while the Engine is working.

IV.

The Engine and Boiler must be supported on Springs, and rest on Six Wheels; and the height from the ground to the top of the Chimney must not exceed Fifteen Feet.

V.

The weight of the Machine, WITH ITS COMPLEMENT OF WATER in the Boiler, must, at most, not exceed Six Tons, and a Machine of less weight will be preferred if it draw AFTER it a PROPORTIONATE weight; and if the weight of the Engine, &c., do not exceed FIVE TONS, then the gross weight to be drawn need not exceed Fifteen Tons; and in that proportion for Machines of still smaller weight—provided that the Engine, &c., shall still be on six wheels, unless the weight (as above) be reduced to Four Tons and a Half, or under, in which case the Boiler, &c., may be placed on four wheels. And the Company shall be at liberty to put the Boiler, Fire Tube, Cylinders, &c., to the test of a pressure of water not exceeding 150 Pounds per square inch, without being answerable for any damage the Machine may receive in consequence.

VI.

There must be a Mercurial Gauge affixed to the Machine, with Index Rod, showing the Steam Pressure above 45 Pounds per square inch; and constructed to blow out a Pressure of 60 Pounds per inch.

VII.

The Engine to be delivered complete for trial, at the Liverpool end of the Railway, not later than the 1st of October next.

VIII.

The price of the Engine which may be accepted, not to exceed £550, delivered on the Railway; and any Engine not approved to be taken back by the Owner.

N.B.—The Railway Company will provide the ENGINE TENDER with a supply of Water and Fuel, for the experiment. The distance within the Rails is four feet eight inches and a half.

THE LOCOMOTIVE STEAM ENGINES.

WHICH COMPETED FOR THE PRIZE OF £500 OFFERED BY THE DIRECTORS OF THE LIVERPOOL AND MANCHESTER RAILWAY COMPANY.

DRAWN TO A SCALE ¼ INCH TO A FOOT.

THE "ROCKET" OF M͏ʳ ROB͏ᵗ STEPHENSON OF NEWCASTLE.

WHICH DRAWING A LOAD EQUIVALENT TO THREE TIMES ITS WEIGHT TRAVELLED AT THE RATE OF 12½ MILES AN HOUR, AND WITH A CARRIAGE & PASSENGERS AT THE RATE OF 24 MILES. COST PER MILE FOR FUEL ABOUT THREE HALF PENCE.

THE "NOVELTY" OF MESS͏ʳˢ BRAITHWAITE & ERRICSSON OF LONDON.

WHICH DRAWING A LOAD EQUIVALENT TO THREE TIMES ITS WEIGHT TRAVELLED AT THE RATE OF 20¾ MILES AN HOUR, AND WITH A CARRIAGE & PASSENGERS AT THE RATE OF 32 MILES. COST PER MILE FOR FUEL ABOUT ONE HALFPENNY.

THE "SANSPAREIL" OF M͏ʳ HACKWORTH OF DARLINGTON.

WHICH DRAWING A LOAD EQUIVALENT TO THREE TIMES ITS WEIGHT TRAVELLED AT THE RATE OF 12½ MILES AN HOUR. COST FOR FUEL PER MILE ABOUT TWO PENCE.

5 Toll-sheet of freight charges for the Surrey Iron Railway. Dated 1 June 1804, this must be one of the very earliest printed railway notices.
Science Museum, London

6 Appropriately lithographed 'by steam power' by Maclure, Macdonald and Macgregor of London, this sheet was issued in 1829 to commemorate the famous locomotive trials at Rainhill. The unorthodox *Novelty* suffered a boiler explosion, *Sanspareil* leaked badly from a defective boiler and cylinder and *Rocket* walked off with the prize of £500. The two last-named are now preserved at the Science Museum in London.
Science Museum, London

colliery lines in the previous decade, it is not surprising that steam power was used for freight services, with horse haulage for passenger trains. On the opening day, though, several hundred wide-eyed guests and company employees were taken for a spin on the line behind *Locomotion*; this historic event was announced a week beforehand in the form of a printed bill giving the itinerary, travelling times and details of festivities. The company took this opportunity 'of enjoining on all their WORK-PEOPLE that attention to *Sobriety* and *Decorum* which they have hitherto had the Pleasure of observing.' Restraint was also exercised in the design of this notice (the Stockton and Darlington was, after all, Quaker-controlled by the Pease family) but the advertisement for the regular passenger service in the *Experiment* coach was much bolder, probably because it was much more overtly commercial in intention than the opening notice (or the Surrey Iron Railway toll-sheet for that matter). The transitional typefaces gave way to more demonstrative fat face display letters, designed by Robert Thorne from the Fann Street typefoundry in London. The *Experiment* itself (horse-drawn of course) was a curious vehicle, resembling a stage coach with flanged wheels, which had taken over from the hut-like vehicle used on the opening day. Note that the coach did not run on Sundays; travelling on the Sabbath was frowned upon in those God-fearing days and a goodly number of vitriolic sermons were successfully preached on this subject in railway districts right up to the end of the Victorian period.

Like the Surrey Iron Railway, the Stockton and Darlington intended that private operators could use their line and therefore permitted them to run passenger-carrying coaches between the two towns. This was an ancient practice, dating back to the old waggonway days when the carriage of coals between pit and loading point was contracted out to a number of competing operators. The arrangement was never a satisfactory one, especially when it coincided with the running of scheduled company trains, and when two cavalcades going in opposite directions met on the same track, an exchange of blows and a consequent disruption of operations was frequent. Even as early as March 1826, the company's management were trying ways of rectifying the situation and this culminated in October 1833 with them taking over the whole of the passenger-carrying operations on the line. By 1827, they had been convinced that steam engines saved something like 30 per cent of the cost per ton-mile when horses were employed, and so the steam locomotive was adopted as the standard form of motive power. These pioneering efforts did not go unnoticed; the Liverpool and Manchester Railway, begun in 1826, took advantage of the Stockton and Darlington's findings to take the railway out of the 'glorified colliery line' category and become the first railway to act as the principal link for all classes of traffic between two large commercial cities. Although the advantages of steam power over the horse were by now widely appreciated, there was still considerable debate between the respective merits of the locomotive engine and the fixed engine, hauling the train over the track by means of a rope. Thus in 1829

the Liverpool and Manchester directors instigated a trial for existing locomotive designs, to be held at Rainhill; Stephenson's *Rocket* walked away with the £500 prize and a lithographed sheet, giving details of the rules and illustrations of the competitors, was issued privately to commemorate the event.

Thus the railway age was ushered in. It owed a lot to the Stephensons: the first public steam-worked railway in France was the Lyon and St Etienne, whose initial locomotives in 1829 were strongly influenced by George Stephenson's ideas. The Paris–St Germain (1837) and two competing lines between Paris and Versailles (1839/40) bought engines from the Stephenson works in Newcastle. George Stephenson went to Spain and Robert to Norway to lay out those countries' first main-line railways, and subsequently British men and machines went out to Germany, Italy, Holland, Belgium, Switzerland, Austria, Russia, America and indeed to almost every part of the world which felt the need for adopting this new revolutionary form of transport. Naturally, efforts had to be made by the railway companies to give details of their services and to make a society, still in part governed by the natural time of job duration or sunrise and sunset, aware that the railway was run by clock time. Perhaps it is for this reason that the bulk of early printed notices from railway companies were less concerned with promotional activities than with communicating and stressing facts to the travelling public. Railway operation was, and still is, complex and orderly; a train has to leave at a certain time and if it does not, then it may well disturb the progress of other trains which are to use the same track. An agricultural worker of this period, say, whose working life was not programmed by factory hooters or time clocks, could not automatically be guaranteed to realise that the railway was run to the far more precise notion of clock time. Nothing on the scale and complexity of the railway had ever been experienced before, and if the London and Birmingham Railway's notice of *circa* 1839 advising that 'Gentlemen's Carriages and Horses must be at the Stations at least a Quarter of an Hour before the time of Departure' smacked of pedantry, then this was very essential pedantry. Railway operation, as the Stockton and Darlington had found out, had to be most carefully planned if chaos and a general free-for-all were not to be the end product, and the travelling public thus had an important responsibility in maintaining this.

The energies of those concerned with producing information had perforce to go into making their notices as clear and unambiguous as possible; there was no room for florid slogan-mongering or other distracting ballyhoo. The design of printed matter (usually entrusted to an outside printer from information supplied by the railway) was therefore straightforward and utilitarian to avoid confusion. The timetable is a classic example of this need to present information in a precise manner, open (or so it was intended!) to only one interpretation. Such notices were posted in the station or depot precincts, or displayed at the offices of railway agents; there seems to be little evidence from the pre-1890 period that railways ever took advantage of sites away from their own premises. Indeed, the whole tenor of printed material of this period is that it is for the consumption of people who have already resolved to travel on or send goods by the railway, a captive audience one might say; there was little or no attempt to lure the prospective customer from outside. There were occasions, though, when the railway notice did go outside: when a new line was to be built, for example, the area to be served would be saturated with notices proposing the scheme. In the Great Western Museum at Swindon there is an amusing reminder that such schemes did not always meet with the full approval of the locals. 'Beware of the Great Western Railway!' is the heading of this notice put out by a local anti-railway pressure group, and it goes on to alert the populace to the dangers of railway scouts in their midst. The usual cause of such hostility was the desire by landowners to milk the encroaching company of every penny it could get for

7 Early commercial railway advertisements were primarily concerned with communicating the essential complexities of railway operation to the public rather than promotional ballyhoo. This toll sheet of *circa* 1839 from the newly opened London and Birmingham Railway is almost obsessively precise in the information it imparts. At this time, private carriages were still being carried (complete with occupants) on railway flat trucks.
British Transport Museum (B Sharpe)

London & Birmingham
RAILWAY.

RATES OF CARRIAGES & HORSES.

TO AND FROM		CARRIAGES.		HORSES.
		4 Wheels	2 Wheels	Each.
London and	**Birmingham** and			
Berkhampstd.	**Rugby** . . .	**20s.**	**15s.**	**20s.**
Wolverton .	**Wolverton** .	**35s.**	**25s.**	**30s.**
Rugby . . .	**Berkhampst**d.	**55s.**	**40s.**	**42s.**
Birmingham .	**London** . . .	**75s.**	**55s.**	**50s.**
		No. 1.	**No. 2.**	

The charge for intermediate distances is in the same proportion as the above rates, but no less rate than 20s. and 15s for any distance.

The same rates are charged for both two and four wheels, as per No. 1 ; and when two vehicles can be placed on one truck, as per No 2.

N. B. Gentlemen's Carriages and Horses must be at the Stations at least a Quarter of an Hour before the time of Departure.

A supply of Trucks will be kept at the principal Stations on the Line ; but, to prevent disappointment, it is recommended that previous notice should be given at the Station where they may be required.

Passengers travelling in or on Gentlemen's Carriages, as well as Grooms in care of Horses, are charged Second Class Fare.

No Horses can be taken by a First Class Train, except when they belong to a Carriage or Passenger accompanying such Train, or to Gentlemen who are travellers by it.

HORSES.

The London and Birmingham Railway Company give Notice that they will not, under any circumstance, be answerable for injury to Horses conveyed upon their Railway; and they will not receive any Horse for conveyance unless accompanied by a Declaration, signed by the Owner or his authorized Agent, that the Company are not to be liable for injury to such Horse while in their custody.

LEEDS & SELBY RAILWAY.

DIMENSIONS OF
WAGGONS
TO BE USED FOR
LIME & COAL.

The Waggons are to be built with double Soles, and are to carry Three Tons when loaded level with the top rails.

		ft. in.	in.	in.
Soles.	Outside, 9 9 long		7 ×	4¼
	Inside,		6 ×	4
		ft.	in.	
Wheels.—	Diameter exclusive of Flange	3	0	
	Guage in the clear,	4	7½	
	Cone, not more than	–	¼	
	Breadth of Tread,	–	3½	
	Do. of Flange,	–	1	
	Height of Do.	–	1	
Axles.	Diameter not less than	–	3¼	
	Journals (outside) Do.	–	2¼	
	Apart from Center to Center, not more than	5	0	

Springs. Three feet long, properly tempered, and to consist of at least, Nine Plates, and to have four inches clear play when unloaded.

Coupling Chains.— Two to each Waggon, one inch round Iron of the best Quality, with strong Hooks.

Grease Bores' and Breaks. To be such as shall be approved by the Engineer to the Company; every Waggon to be provided with one of the latter.

Draw Bars. Three inches by one inch, with strong eye for Chain Hook, turned up at end, and firmly secured to the framing of the Waggon.

The whole of the Wrought Iron described, to be of the best Scrap Bars; the Wheels to be of the best Yorkshire castings.

Every Waggon to be numbered, and to have the name of the Owner painted on it in two inch letters; none to be used on the Railway without being previously examined by a Person appointed by the Railway Company for that purpose.

FREDFRICK HOBSON, PRINTER, TIMES-OFFICE, LEEDS.

8

14

the sale of land; a concerted display of opposition might well cause the railway to increase their offer to avoid a protracted legal battle for land. Then again, in an age when railways were not economically integrated, and had to rely on outside builders for such fittings as engines, rolling stock and rails, circulars were sent around the various manufacturers to invite tenders for the supply of these essentials. Manufacturers, in turn, issued their own advertisements in the trade press. The bulk of railway advertising outside railway premises was carried by newspapers, both local and national, and this resulted in a practice which was soon taken up in the production of printed posters, namely the incorporation of a woodcut illustration into the text of the advertisement.

9

The proliferation of woodcut illustrations in the advertising of the 1840s, a cheap but effective way of drawing attention to the substance of the notice, can largely be attributed to the efforts of Thomas Bewick (1753-1828). Apprenticed in his teens to a Newcastle engraver specialising in etching ornamental silver and billheads, Bewick was entrusted with occasional requests for wood-engravings. He mastered the techniques involved to such effect that he was awarded seven guineas by the Society for the Encouragement of the Arts for his block 'The Huntsman and the Old Hound'. This encouraged him to try to improve on the traditional and rather heavy current technique, pioneered in Germany, of graving on the plank of the wood. By graving on the end of the wood instead, he found he could produce cheap, detailed and durable blocks for such work as book illustration, business and trade cards, letterheads and tailpieces. His fame rests largely with his sensitive but homely illustrations for the *General History of Quadrupeds* (1797) and the two-volume *History of British Birds*, first published in 1804. However, in terms of making the printing and dissemination of cheap illustrated material much more widely available to the general public than had ever been possible with copper engravings, his contribution to the spread of literacy and good taste was immense. Indeed, until photo-engraving became practical in the 1880s, the Bewick method of wood-engraving was the principal method of book, periodical and advertisement illustration for the better part of a century.

Not surprisingly, therefore, those concerned with creating promotional railway material in the railway mania days in Britain and abroad made full use of the woodcut block. It gave pleasing results, cost little to produce and would obviously draw the traveller's attention much more easily than a bald typographical announcement. As has been remarked, the railway company supplied the copy and it was left to the printer to work up an appealing design for the poster. These Victorian printers had available to them a wide range of blocks of locomotives and trains from the catalogues of the block-making firms. These were rarely, if ever, authentic representations of any particular company's stock and consequently a block used for a notice put out by one company was quite likely to be used by a second printer for another company's advertising in a different part of the country. Since the blocks made on the Bewick principle were exceedingly durable (some of his original woodcuts were capable of withstanding some 900,000 impressions) it is by no means uncommon to find a block showing a train of the 1840s still anachronistically in use on notices, and especially in newspaper advertisements, until well into the last quarter of the century, by which time the prototype had altered beyond all recognition.

As can be seen from the accompanying illustrations of blocks used in different countries for poster and newspaper advertising, these woodcuts varied considerably in quality and representational worth, though the type of train depicted was usually of an identifiable national type, such as the American engines with their spacious cabs and pilots at the front. There were two main methods of using these blocks. One was to take a view of the entire train; this could either be a straightforward side elevation, or a perspective view with the train in a scenic setting. The latter approach was sometimes varied, if there was a suitable building in the picture, by stripping in the name of a station mentioned in the text of the notice in an appropriate position on the illustration. The other technique, which can be clearly seen in an advertisement for a special train on the Newcastle and Carlisle Railway issued in 1846, was to build the whole train from a number of separate blocks each depicting, say, the engine, the tender, a first-class coach, a third-class coach and so on, until the desired effect was achieved.

8 A bill issued in 1836 by the Leeds and Selby Railway specifying the permitted dimensions for privately owned goods vehicles carried on the railway.
Science Museum, London

9 1866 advertisement from the Yorkshire wagon-building firm of Charles Roberts, still in existence today.
Charles Roberts & Co Ltd

10 Examples of blocks used for the woodcut illustration of railway advertising material in the 1840s, from contemporary block makers' pattern books. Blocks like these could often be found in use long after the actual trains depicted had been withdrawn.

11 The elaborate design of this notice of 1842 for a public demonstration of Robert Davidson's electric locomotive contrasts strongly with the more utilitarian posters issued by railway companies in the early Victorian years. The locomotive was intended for a line between Glasgow and Edinburgh.
Science Museum, London

12 After the timetable, the most familiar railway notice is probably the trespass warning. This 1835 example from the Newcastle and Carlisle Railway employs the standard handbill format, although in later years cast-iron notices were almost universally employed to keep people off the line. Note the severity of the punishment for convicted trespassers.
Science Museum, London

ELECTRO-MAGNETIC
EXHIBITION,
UNDER THE PATRONAGE OF THE
Royal Scottish Society of Arts.

Mr. ROBERT DAVIDSON'S
EXHIBITION OF ELECTRO-MAGNETISM,
AS A MOVING POWER,
IS NOW OPEN!
IN THE
EGYPTIAN HALL, Piccadilly.

THE MODELS AND APPARATUS COMPRISE THE FOLLOWING:
A LOCOMOTIVE ENGINE,
Carrying Passengers on a CIRCULAR RAILWAY.
A PRINTING MACHINE AND TURNING LATHE.
A SAW MILL.
A MACHINE for COMMUNICATING the ELECTRO-MAGNETIC SHOCK.
AN ELECTRO-MAGNET!
The largest ever made. It weighs upwards of 500 Pounds, and will suspend many Tons.
A GALVANIC TELEGRAPH.
THE COMBUSTION OF METALS,
Attended in each case with Splendid Coruscations, peculiar in color to the Metal operated upon, &c &c.

10 000 small Nails formed into a Rope)

Balloon Navigation Illustrated.

MODEL OF THE FLYING MACHINE
MODEL OF AN ÆRIAL CARRIAGE,
By Sir GEORGE CAYLEY.

OPEN FROM 12 TILL 6, AND FROM 7 TILL 9.
Admission, ONE SHILLING.
Children under 12 Years of Age, SIXPENCE.
PRINTED BY ELECTRO-MAGNETISM.

NEWCASTLE
AND
CARLISLE
Railway.

Notice is hereby Given,

THAT all Persons trespassing on the Railway, or the Works thereof, are liable *to a considerable Penalty* for each Offence. And that the Punishment for doing any Injury or Damage to the said Railway is

Transportation for 7 Years.

THE DIRECTORS GIVE THIS PUBLIC

WARNING,

that they are determined to Prosecute with the utmost Rigour, all Persons who may do any such Injury or Damage to the Railway; and that positive Orders are given to all the Servants of the Company, to give Information against any Persons trespassing thereon.

JOHN ADAMSON,
Clerk to the Company.

Railway Office, Newcastle upon Tyne,
21st August, 1835.

Akenheads, Printers, Newcastle

12

NEWCASTLE and CARLISLE RAILWAY

Carlisle Races
AND
WRESTLING.

A SPECIAL TRAIN

Will leave the NEWCASTLE STATION on the Morning of

Wednesday, July 1st,

At EIGHT o'clock, for Carlisle, taking up Passengers at all the Stations; who may return by any of the Regular Trains (except the Mail Trains) until Friday Evening, the 3d of July. Parties from North Shields, &c., will be allowed to proceed by the Train leaving Newcastle at Nine o'clock in the Morning of July 1.

Fares, from Newcastle to Carlisle and back,

First Class, **11s.** | Second Class, **8s. 6d.** | Third Class, **5s.**

And in proportion from all the other Stations.——By order,

JOHN ADAMSON,
Clerk to the Company.

Railway Office, Forth, Newcastle, June 17, 1846.

PRINTED BY WILLIAM DOUGLAS, OBSERVER OFFICE, HIGH STREET, GATESHEAD.

13 Newcastle and Carlisle Railway excursion poster of 1846, using a side-elevation woodcut made up from several blocks in train-set style.
British Transport Museum (B Sharpe)

1880. 1880.
CHEAPEST EXCURSION
OF THE SEASON
Under the Auspices of the
St. Andrew's Society of Kingston

BY GRAND TRUNK RAILWAY,
FROM KINGSTON
TO MONTREAL
AND RETURN.
CIVIC HOLIDAY,
Wednesday, August 18th.

Train will leave foot of Brock Street at 6 o'clock A.M., sharp.
TICKETS, Round Trip, $2.00.
Further particulars in a few days.
W. G. CRAIG, PRESIDENT.   JAS. YULE, SECRETARY.

15

GREAT NORTHERN RAILWAY.

The **PUBLIC** is respectfully informed that in consequence of the Trains of the GREAT NORTHERN RAILWAY COMPANY having been prevented from proceeding to LEEDS by the METHLEY JUNCTION, they will run between DONCASTER, WAKEFIELD, NORMANTON, and LEEDS, by the LANCASHIRE AND YORKSHIRE RAILWAY as follows, until further Notice; and that in all other respects the Trains will correspond with the published Time Bills.

Superintendent's Office, Lincoln,   BY ORDER,
4th September, 1849.   JOHN DENNISTON.

ROBERT HARTLEY, PRINTER, HIGH-STREET, DONCASTER.

---

14 A late example of the perspective view type of woodcut, incorporated into an excursion handbill of 1880. Note the starting time and the ridiculously cheap fare for the distance to be covered.
Canadian National Railway (Historical Projects Branch)

---

15 This Great Northern Railway poster, dated 4 September 1849, uses the more conventional one-piece block. Engines at either end of the train were more common in excursion working than in normal main-line running. The alterations to the scheduled services were probably caused by a squabble with a rival company over whose lines the Great Northern exercised running rights. Such conflicts were by no means uncommon in the Railway Mania days and sometimes resulted in the confiscation of whole trains and the tearing up of track.
British Transport Museum (B Sharpe)

---

16 Notice of 1845 advising the populace of the intended construction of the Montreal and Lachine Railway.
Canadian National Railway (Historical Projects Branch)

Whichever method was used, be it single or composite blocks, it cannot be said that any great effort was made to integrate illustration and text into a harmonious whole. Each was the work of a separate person, and it was not until the full-scale advent of colour-lithographed posters in the 1890s that an actual poster designer, rather than the compositor, became responsible for the effective marriage of these two elements. The mid-century compositors tended to lay out the woodcut illustration as a substitute for a line of display letters and failed to see its own possibilities as the basis for the design. One need only compare the Union Pacific's 'Shortest and Quickest Route between the Mountains and the East' poster of 1867 with the same company's 'Through Kansas & Nebraska to the Rockies and Beyond' of a quarter-century later to realise how effective the correlation of typographical design to illustration and vice-versa could be.

Where it was not deemed necessary to incorporate a woodcut into the poster, the inventive powers of the compositor in choosing typefaces were taxed to the full. The methodical setting-out of information in a clear and precise way which had characterised the railway notices of the 1840s, was abandoned after a few utilitarian years, in favour of a veritable blitz of different types. The Union Pacific poster of 1867 mentioned above had, in addition to the woodcut and a pair of those curiously Victorian pointing hands, no less than twenty-three different faces for twenty-nine lines of text. A Canadian Pacific poster of the same period for land explorers' excursions to Manitoba and the north-west boasted twenty-odd different typefaces in the English language version, and a similar number – but almost all completely different! – for the French variety. Ranging from fat-face to the miniscule, such posters had more in common with opticians' test cards than publicity material; judging by the length of time it takes to read these posters, they clearly belong to a more leisured age than our own, where modern advertising agents claim that any poster which cannot be taken in within two seconds is utterly ineffective.

Before moving on to look at the pictorial posters which came in in the 1890s to offer (presumably) a

NOTICE   16
IS HEREBY GIVEN,
That application will be made at the next Session of Parliament, for an Act to Incorporate certain persons to construct
A RAILWAY
FROM
Montreal to Lachine,
UNDER THE NAME AND DESIGNATION OF
THE MONTREAL AND LACHINE RAILWAY COMPANY.
Lachine, 1st November, 1845

THE SHORTEST AND QUICKEST ROUTE
BETWEEN THE
MOUNTAINS AND THE EAST
IS VIA THE

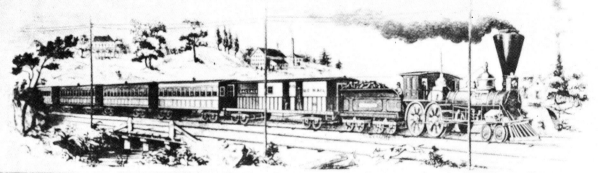

UNION PACIFIC R.R
NOW OPEN FROM
OMAHA TO NORTH PLATTE
300 Miles West of the Missouri River, and 200 Miles nearer Denver and Salt Lake than any other Railroad Line.

All Passenger Trains of this Road Connect Direct
WITH TRAINS OF THE
CHICAGO & NORTH-WESTERN R'Y, WHICH IS NOW COMPLETED FROM
CHICAGO TO OMAHA
Making 800 Miles of Railroad directly West of Chicago with but "One Change of Cars."

PASSENGERS CROSSING THE PLAINS
Will save 200 Miles Stage Travel and 48 Hours Time by taking this Route.
PULLMAN'S PALACE SLEEPING CARS ON ALL NIGHT TRAINS
Equipment all new, and Road bed in perfect order. Good Eating Houses at convenient points on line.

DIRECT CONNECTIONS MADE AT NORTH PLATTE WITH WELLS, FARGO & CO'S DAILY LINES OF
OVERLAND MAIL AND EXPRESS COACHES
To and from Denver, Central City, Salt Lake, and ALL POINTS in Colorado, Utah, Idaho, Montana, Nevada and California.

PASSENGERS, TO AVAIL THEMSELVES OF THE QUICK TIME AND SURE CONNECTIONS OF THIS ROUTE, MUST
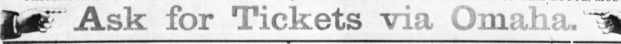
Ask for Tickets via Omaha.

THE ATTENTION OF SHIPPERS OF FREIGHT FOR THE MOUNTAINS
Is particularly called to the opening of the great Platte Valley Route to NORTH PLATTE, and its connections. 200 Miles of Wagon Transportation is saved in sending Goods via OMAHA. Reliable Freight Lines are at all times prepared to transport Goods from the Western terminus of this Road to all points in the Mountains. Careful handling and quick time guaranteed.
RATES ALWAYS AS LOW AND CHANGES FEWER THAN BY ANY OTHER ROUTE.

W. SNYDER, Gen'l Fr't and Ticket Agent.   **SAM'L B. REED,** Gen'l Superintendent.

Omaha, March 9th, 1867.

17

18

19

17 Union Pacific Railroad poster dated 8 March 1867, employing a perspective illustration and twenty-three different typefaces. Such typographical extravaganzas probably confused more travellers than they enlightened.
Union Pacific Railroad Museum collection

18 Poster advertising the opening of the Union Pacific's Platte Valley route between Omaha and San Francisco in 1869, forming the first transcontinental railroad in the United States. The elk was to become a famous trade mark, one of the very first logos to be used by a railway company.
Union Pacific Railroad Museum collection

19 Long-distance excursion running frequently involved the co-operation of several companies. This poster for a special train to the Garibaldi demonstration at the Crystal Palace in April 1864 was jointly issued by the Midland and North Eastern companies. In addition to display lettering, a frequent device to attract attention to typographical posters was to print on coloured paper.
British Transport Museum (B Sharpe)

much-needed respite from these dazzling and confusing displays, we should briefly consider how the railway companies went about the business of advertising at this time. By the 1870s, the bulk of our present railway network (or rather that which existed before the severe economic pruning of the post-war years got under way) had, thanks to the efforts of Messrs Stephenson, Hudson, Brassey, Locke, Peto and Betts, been completed in most parts of the world. In addition to the considerable volume of traffic which it had won from the canals, the railway had, by a cause and effect process, acquired almost all the freight transport in and between the industrialised areas. Passenger travel was on a scale and social distribution which had never been seen before; for the carriage of such important matters as mail and newspapers, the railway was the most important medium of communication in the world. It was a situation of almost complete monopoly; not surprisingly, therefore, there was a strong element of complacency. There was no need to go out and court potential traffic, for there was more than enough flocking willingly on to the trains already. Thus the desperately competitive element, so strong at the close of the century when the general economic trough caused the companies to realise their pointless duplication of other companies' routes and made them fight for the diminishing traffic, was almost totally lacking. In terms of the language in which advertising was couched (America was a possible exception here) prosaic factual statements still held sway; this forms an interesting comparison with the more colourful, slogan-oriented rhetoric of the stage-coach days, where the elements of competition and rivalry were much more keenly felt. The vim characteristic of the later seaside railway poster can be seen, in retrospect, to be markedly absent, although it must be pointed out that an annual holiday by the sea was still beyond the means of the average working family and so the railway companies were not yet ready to exploit this facet of travel in their services and advertising. By and large, then, the companies were content to do very little in the way of creative promotion, and concentrated instead on keeping the public informed of such matters as train times and fares, excursion trains, new stations or lines and alterations to existing services.

Very little information seems to be available about the actual organisation of advertising at this time, but R. B. Wilson, in his excellent *Go Great Western: A History of GWR Publicity*, has unearthed some very valuable details of this company's activities which can serve as an example. Prior to 1870 the GWR had employed an advertising agent; this seems to have been a rare practice, and indeed the majority of posters from this period carry the names of directors and superintendents in preference to those of outside agents. What is certain, though, is that a great number of contemporary bills were commissioned by local officials and handed to local jobbing printers without reference to head office. The net result of this rather amateurish process was that it is very difficult to tell from first impressions

Credit Valley Railway

Running in Connection with Port Dover Railway.

NO. 2 TIME TABLE. NO. 2.

Taking effect Monday, 9th September, 1878.

Miles	GOING EAST. No.1	No.3	STATIONS.			GOING WEST. No.2	No.4	Miles
	A.M.	P.M.				A.M.	P.M.	
0	7.40	4.00	Dep.	Ingersoll.	Arr.	9.15	5.25	10
2	7.45	4.05		× Centreville.		9.10	5.20	8
5	7.55	4.15		Beachville.		9.00	5.10	5
10	8.10	4.30		Woodstock.		8.45	4.55	0
—	8.15	4.35	Arr.	Woodstock, P.D.&L.H.R'y.	Dep.	8.40	4.50	—

× Flag Station—Will stop on signal.

C. LAIDLAW,

September, 1878. Managing Director.

20

20 One of the most familiar methods of passing on information on train services has always been the timetable. This refreshingly simple timetable, with two trains in each direction daily, comes from the Credit Valley Railway in Ontario.
CP Rail

21 Theoretically straightforward, the railway timetable could in practice become bewilderingly complicated, as with this South Eastern Railway timetable dated 1 July 1846.
British Transport Museum (B Sharpe)

21

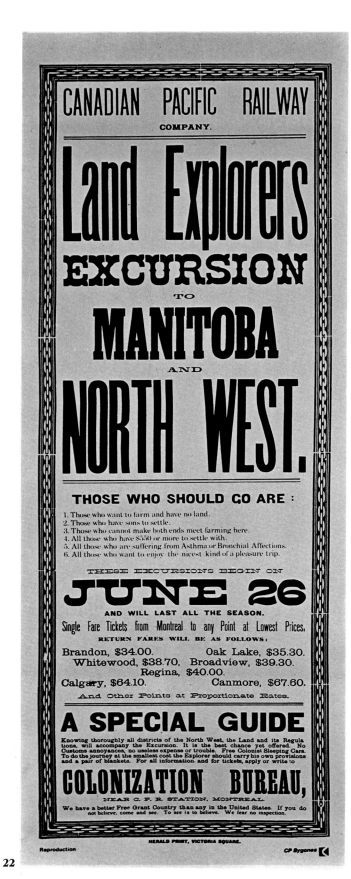

22

23

22, 23 Two versions of the same Canadian Pacific poster, one in English and the other in French. The enthusiasm of the compositor has led him to set virtually every corresponding line in a different face.
CP Rail

whether or not any two posters actually came from the same company, so great is the difference in styles and approaches adopted. Around 1870, Wilson tells us, the GWR began to instigate a more thorough-going attitude towards publicity. The outside agent was replaced by a clerk at the general manager's office at Paddington in charge of advertising, and two men were employed to go around the system to see that the bills sent out by the advertising clerk and his assistant were correctly displayed. Bill inspectors were common on all major railways at this time, so the Great Western seems to have been a little backward here. The practice of the local printing of bills was still continued, however, and the Paddington office was responsible only for preparing guide books (a very inventive and lucrative form of publicity at this time) and the advertisements which were to appear in the London press and in periodicals. It was

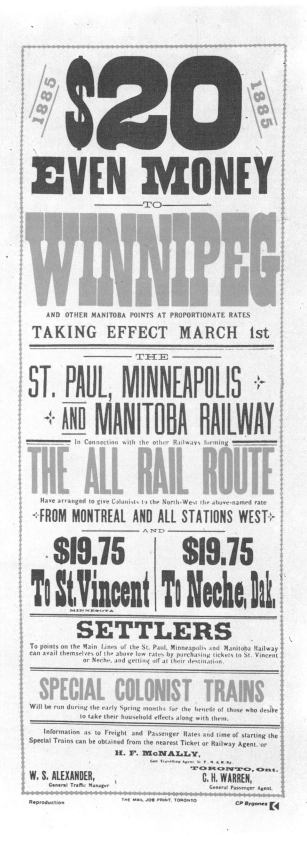

24 Poster from the Passumpsic Railroad, advertising special concessionary fares in force on Independance Day, 1876. *CP Rail*

not until 1886 that a separate advertising department was formed (initially with only six clerks) to have some degree of co-ordinating control over the divided efforts in what was now realised to be the very valuable area of publicity. The amount of money spent on advertising rose appreciably at the close of the nineteenth century, from £5,952 in 1888 to £9,134 ten years later, but by 1901 it had dropped to £6,781, by which time, as we shall see, the Great Western had become very much a back-marker in the publicity stakes.

25-8 A selection of Canadian posters from the mid 1880s, showing the continued popularity of full face display letters over eighty years after their introduction to the field of advertising.
CP Rail

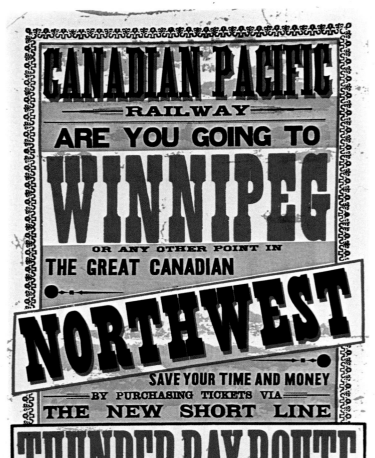

29 Not perhaps the greatest poster design of the 1890s, but this Union Pacific poster reveals that all design, engraving and printing was handled by an outside contractor, in this case the Buffalo *Morning Express*, rather than by the railway company itself. This was a common practice at the time.
Union Pacific Railroad Museum collection

30 The beginnings of integration of typography and graphics can be seen in the design of this Union Pacific poster of *circa* 1890-3. Besides the obvious implications of a better life in the west, travel through the Rockies held considerable attraction for the travelling public. Note that the elk is still going strong.
Union Pacific Railroad Museum collection

31 As with the Canadian posters above, the way west was the basis of much North American advertising in the nineteenth century after the major routes had been opened up. Railroad companies often doubled as land dealers, as in this poster of *circa* 1892 advertising the sale of 700,000 acres of prime Kansas farming land by the Union Pacific.
Kansas State Historical Society

32 A bizarre Canadian Pacific poster of 1893 advertising holiday tours at home and abroad through the grotesque parody of racial and social archetypes.
CP Rail

31

32

WELLAND RAILWAY
PASSENGER
TIME TABLE
No. 10,
TO COMMENCE MONDAY, APRIL 15th, 1861.

GOING SOUTH. | GOING NORTH.

	No. 1.	No. 3.	‡ACCOM		‡ACCOM	No. 2.	No. 4.
	A.M.	P.M.	P.M.		A.M.	A.M.	P.M.
†P't Dalhousie,	7.30	1.30	4.30	Buffalo, (LEAVE.) *	......	10.40	2.00
†St. Catharines,	7.50	1.50	4.50	Port Colborne	8.30	11.30	4.30
†Thorold,	8.15	2.15	5.15	Welland,	8.45	11.50	4.50
Allanburgh, FLAG	8.25	2.25	5.25	Port Robinson	9.02	12.02	5.02
†Port Robinson	8.33	2.33	5.33	Allanburgh, FLAG	9.10	12.10	5.10
†Welland,	8.45	2.45	5.45	Thorold,	9.20	12.20	5.20
†Port Colborne,	9.10	3.10	6.10	St. Catharines	9.40	12.40	5.40
†Buffalo, ARRIVE, *	11.45	5.40	......	P't Dalhousie,	10.00	1.00	6.00

* New-York Time, all other Hamilton Time.   † Telegraph Stations.   ‡ Accommodation Train will commence on 1st May.

The Company will not be responsible for the hours of departure and arrival, nor for the regularity of the Trains of other Companies, as given in this Table; the connections their Trains are expected to make are only shown for the convenience of Passengers.

CORNELIUS STOVIN,
ST. CATHARINES, April 15, 1861.   General Manager.

ST. CATHARINES "HERALD" PRINT.

33 Generally speaking, the timetables of the mid-nineteenth century were laid out in a basic and unpretentious way, but this Welland Railway table of 1861 features a tasteful decorative border. Note that, while most of the trains run to Hamilton (Ontario) time, departures and arrivals at Buffalo are in New York time. The problems of different time-zones were not immediately apparent until the railway age.
Canadian National Railway (Historical Projects Branch)

Chapter Two

Fast and Frequent Services to all Parts...

By 1890, the old typographical railway notice had virtually been exhausted as an advertising medium. Whilst it may well convey to us a strong period sense, we are fortunate that we, unlike our great-grandparents, did not have to draw our travel information from it; these Victorian extravaganzas probably confused more intending travellers than they enlightened. At this time, competition between rival companies for passengers (often between the same towns but by different routes) had become much more intense than it had ever been in the comparatively sedate 1870s. New approaches to advertising were needed, and the full-scale advent of the lithographic poster at this time offered a heaven-sent opportunity to the sorely pressed advertising departments of railway companies to cajole potential ticket-buyers.

Lithography was nothing new in the last decade of the nineteenth century. It was invented, or rather fortuitously discovered, by one Aloys Senefelder in 1798 who, so he claimed, discovered the process when trying to write his mother's laundry list on a piece of stone with a greasy pencil. He saw the possibilities of chipping away the stone and leaving the markings in relief, which, when coated with a greasy (i.e. water-repellant) ink, could be used to obtain a reverse impression on paper. Further experimentation proved that this was a workable proposition and so, especially in France and England, Senefelder's discovery was put to commercial use. Since the process of colour lithography was a far more complex and costly source of illustration than the engraved block method, involving the creation of a master black

34

stone and four distinct applications of stones covered with red, yellow, black and blue pigment, it was of necessity limited in its application. At first the process was restricted to such work as the printing of bookseller's handbills, where enlarged book illustrations were used to promote the latest novels, but once zinc plates had begun to replace the stone blocks (some three or four inches thick, and requiring to be ground down before the next print run could be made with a different design) lithography achieved a wider distribution.

Jules Chéret came across a modernised version of Senefelder's equipment in England in 1870 and, back in Paris, adapted it for his influential 'Bal Valentino' poster of 1872. By the early 1890s his work, together with that of such masters of the poster as Toulouse Lautrec, de Feure, Steinlen and Mucha, had completely revolutionised advertising design. Gone were the stuffy and pompous messages, the dull layers of type and the cramped wood-engravings. In their place came integrated layouts of text and picture, bright colours, bold, flat outlines and seductive female figures who totally dominated the far more prosaic cigarette paper or paraffin oil they were meant to be promoting. As one distinguished poster historian has observed, whilst Chéret may not have invented the pin-up, to him is certainly attributable the paste-up! The changing nature of the central female figure is certainly one which will occupy us later in this chapter.

Almost overnight, Paris (then undergoing substantial rebuilding, and, with miles of temporary walling surrounding the works-in-progress, a haven for bill-posters) became festooned with these vivid examples of popular art. In her definitive *The French Poster: Chéret to Cappiello*, Jane Abdy incorporates an appropriate quotation from Ernest Maindron, made in 1895; 'Each new day which dawns, all Paris, and also the provinces, find themselves on waking surrounded by original works of art, which are delightful to look at, and in which the craftsmanship equals the charm.' Railway companies, in the rest of Europe as well as in France, were quick to seize on the eye-catching properties of the full-colour pictorial poster. Though Toulouse Lautrec is rumoured to have included a small number of railway posters in his prodigious output of the last few years of the nineteenth century, these have remained elusive to researchers. In fact big names in French poster design figure only very rarely as the signatures on the railway posters of the period. This may be attributable to the lack of inspiration they found in the subject (for the presence of a product was secondary to their artistic designs – many in fact used existing designs in their notebooks when commissioned for commercial work), or to the conservatism of their railway patrons who laid down hard and fast rules as to what should go into a poster (a Moulin Rouge-style girl was hardly a suitable subject for a poster for the prosaic Chemins de Fer de l'Ouest!) A more likely explanation is that the railway companies were simply unwilling to spend the considerable sums which artists like Mucha in France, Will Bradley in America and Privat-Livemont in

Belgium were able to command. By 1900 few companies were able, like the efficient and ambitious Lancashire and Yorkshire Railway in the north of England, to allocate £7,000 per annum to publicity work, and they could hardly have offered advances to attract the attention of the poster masters. Even as famous and instantly successful a poster as John Hassall's 'Skegness is So Bracing' commanded the meagre fee of £12 for its designer from the Great Northern Railway.

So the railway companies paid their money and took their chance; the artist Gunn Gwennet, commenting in 1900 on railway posters in general, felt that the majority of companies did not get value for their money in their posters, partly because a number still relied on the bald typographical announcement, but mainly because the pictures on the majority of railway posters were of inferior quality as works of art. Certainly no one familiar with the magnificent *fin de siècle* work of the maestros we have mentioned

35 Complicated but successful, this Dieppe poster from the Ouest company was one of the very earliest full-colour lithographed French posters. Its inspiration could well have been derived from the famous 'Bubbles' poster for Pear's Soap.
La Vie du Rail

36 Another highly imaginative early French poster issued by the Paris-Lyon-Mediterranée company. Such a strong hint of the 'naughty nineties' would have been far too daring for use on contemporary British posters.
La Vie du Rail

37 A delicate Nord poster of *circa* 1895 by Gustave Fraipont. The way the information panels have been blended in with the whole design is especially commendable. *La Vie du Rail*

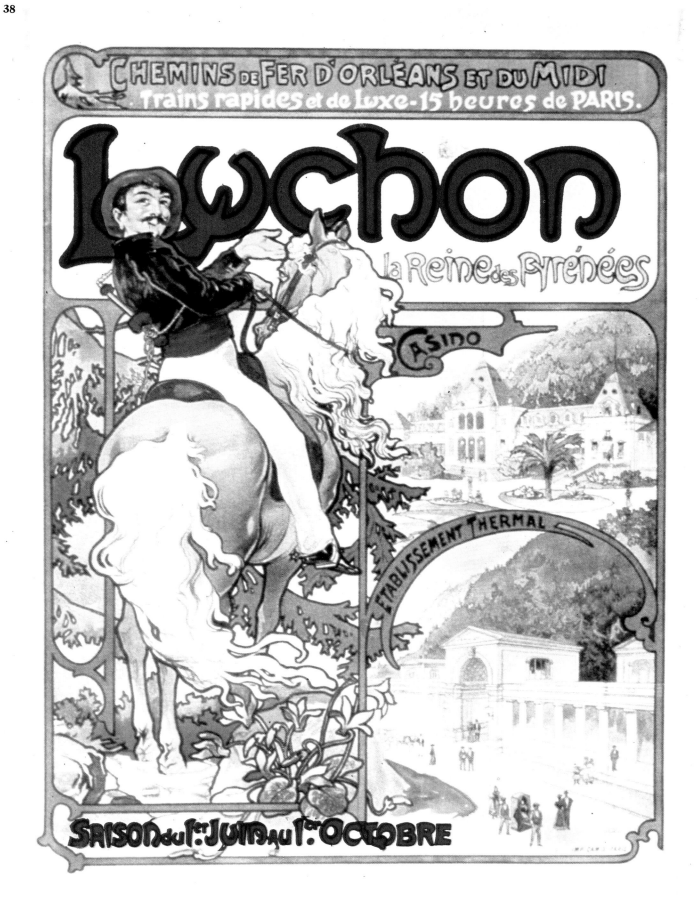

38 Joint Orléans and Midi poster in art nouveau style for the prestigious Pyrenees resort of Bagnères-de-Luchon. The casino seems to receive more stress than the mineral baths!
La Vie du Rail

would lay any great claim on the contemporary railway poster as being a strong example of all that was best in the art of the period. The influence of the Japanese colour print, so strong with the Toulouse Lautrec school, was almost negligible with those who carried out railway commissions. Bold outline and an intelligent use of figures in the composition might be present, but daring colours and the revolutionary relegation of lettering to the background of the design were, with some honourable exceptions, noticeably absent. So too was Impressionism, then, via Cézanne, Renoir, Dégas, Monet, Pisarro and others, creating a whole new concept of light and space. To be fair, this was an area which even the greatest French posterists chose to ignore. From Chéret right down to the humblest hack, the posterists' mentors were, until they discovered the Japanese print, Meissonier and Bouguereau, bourgeois artists of the baroque and rococo. Save for the odd flirtation with art nouveau (a very strong element in the 'Luchon' poster put out by the Chemins de Fer d'Orléans et du Midi), the railway posterists seldom left the safe preserves of representational painting and the sugary, classical female figure.

If the designs which have been passed down to us represent an orthodox approach to pictorial posters, then they are still worthy of consideration as examples of what was typical of the posters in circulation at that time. Certainly the work of Toulouse Lautrec and Mucha was the exception rather than the norm of contemporary poster design; the more naive, less consciously aesthetic approach of the bicycle posters of Pierre Bonnard has long

been of greater interest to a more socially oriented school of thought, and the same techniques and values can equally well be applied to railway posters. Their range and scope is quite exceptional; true, there were some real horrors and a lot of plagiarism, but amongst the dross there lay some real gems.

The subject matter was, at first, somewhat limited. Posters were relatively expensive to produce from four-colour blocks and, as we have seen, turn-of-the-century railway companies were not disposed to allocate lavish budgets to their publicity departments, even assuming that they had been far-sighted enough to create a separate department for promotional activities. For instance, according to Wilson, the cost to the Great Western Railway of printing Alec Fraser's 'Beautiful Britain – Beautiful Brittany' poster of 1907 was £100 for 5,000 quad royal and £105 for 3,000 eight-sheet versions. These prices, while not exorbitant in themselves, still made a fair inroad into the publicity budget and so it seemed to

39 Though a conventional enough landscape view, this Chemins de Fer de l'Est poster by J Hugo Alire promoting the Vosges is of considerable interest in that it shows a primitive sledgeway, a distant ancestor of the railway used for centuries for the transportation of heavy loads in mountain regions.
La Vie du Rail

40 A more genteel poster by F Desportes, issued by the Orleans and Est companies in 1899. Such sugary females were felt to be more appropriate to bourgeois spas and health resorts rather than the voluptuous types used on seaside posters.
La Vie du Rail

39

40

CHEMINS DE FER D'ALSACE ET DE LORRAINE

MONT S^{TE} ODILE

41

be an accepted practice that colour posters were used mainly for advertising those railway services which would continue to enjoy a long-term patronage from the public, such as popular coastal resorts, spas, holiday areas and the like. A single excursion or a special train was still catered for by the distribution and cheaply printed handbills of the type which we have looked at in the previous chapter.

The Midland Railway poster for the popular Lancashire coast holiday town of Blackpool was a typical example of the seaside poster: a general view of the sea frontage, with the twin piers at which steamers for the Isle of Man and the Welsh coast were departing and arriving, was supported by views of the town and esplanade, in one of which the tramway (still in use today) could be seen. The poster can be accurately dated as being late 1890s, since the famous Blackpool Tower, modelled on the Eiffel Tower in Paris, had not yet been erected on the seafront and the bathing machines were still in use. It was a reasonably attractive piece of advertising, especially with the emphatic indentification of the town and the use of the then-current slogan 'Health and Pleasure, Glorious Sea', but it fell victim to a practice which was to bedevil many seaside railway posters in Britain in the years to come. The cost of producing them was shared between the railway company and the resort authorities, and as an additional incentive the latter was also offered a substantial reduction in advertising rates for displays on railway premises. This meant, in practice, that the design, once it had been originated by the railway company, had to meet with the approval of the local council before it could be released. This check on the powers of invention of the artist, by and large, restricted him to representational views which would show the resort to its best advantage (in the eyes of the mayor and his aldermen, that is). Until as late as the 1920s, and sometimes much later, the half-naked bathing belle was much frowned upon, even though Chéret had, from the start, proved that sex was the magic ingredient in the appeal of a poster. And so Blackpool, then as now, a brash, vulgar, noisy and wholly delightful summer refuge for Lancashire mill-workers, came across as a staid and conservative bastion of middle-class respectability; even the church spires on the left of the main picture seemed to have acquired a special prominence.

If the British railway directors seemed to hold shares in the resorts their tracks served (as Maurice Rickards claims in his *Posters at the Turn of the Century*), and thus a vested interest in bowing to the narrow tastes of seaside authorities, then the same does not hold true to anything like the same degree in Europe. There, poster designers seem to have had a much freer hand, and many memorably inventive designs resulted. The Ouest and Paris-Lyon-Mediterranée companies especially were responsible for some of the better work which came out of the 1890s, and two examples are illustrated. The PLM's 'Côte d'Azur' poster was a whirling fantasy of light and colour, where a buxom Parisian sophisticate in a froth of pure Chéret petticoats danced gaily (scattering money!) above an alluring coastline, while

yachts sailed on the clear waters and a motor-car (the very symbol of progress and adventure) added its own trailing cloud of dust to the vortex in the centre of the picture. The daring glimpse of ankle would most probably have induced fits in the worthy Blackpool dignitaries; they might have been appeased somewhat by the Ouest company's 'L'Été à Dieppe' poster. This would seem to pre-date the 'Côte d'Azur' poster, since, as well as the presence of a motor-car in the latter, the Ouest poster bore more than a passing resemblance to the popular 'Bubbles' poster of 1889 *et seq* which Thomas Barratt – wily entrepreneur that he was – had cunningly pirated for Pear's soap from Sir John Millais' famous painting. Promotional views of the town were there, but one

understands first the motif of the group of children blowing bubbles before previewing the delights of 'La Seule Plage à 3hrs de Paris'.

In both these designs, the lettering was woven in harmoniously with the whole (so harmoniously, that one scarcely notices it in the PLM poster) but this concentration on pictorial appeal, though the hallmark of the top French designers, was not altogether typical of contemporary railway advertising. Just as in earlier years the railway authorities had felt obliged to cram masses of typographical information into their posters and handbills, so they continued to do when they began to use full pictorial advertising. Faced with the necessity of incorporating factual information when they were really more interested

41 A beautiful and curiously three-dimensional scenic design by L Blumer for the Chemins de Fer d'Alsace et de Lorraine.
La Vie du Rail

42 A typical mid-1890s British seaside poster, produced by Bemrose and Sons of Derby and London jointly for the Midland Railway (centred on Derby) and the Lancashire coast resort of Blackpool. Such co-operation between local authorities and railway companies became extremely popular in the years immediately prior to World War I. Blackpool was one of the very first in this field, and enjoyed cheap advertising rates on the railway, while the Midland reaped the benefits of the extra traffic the posters encouraged.
British Transport Museum (B Sharpe)

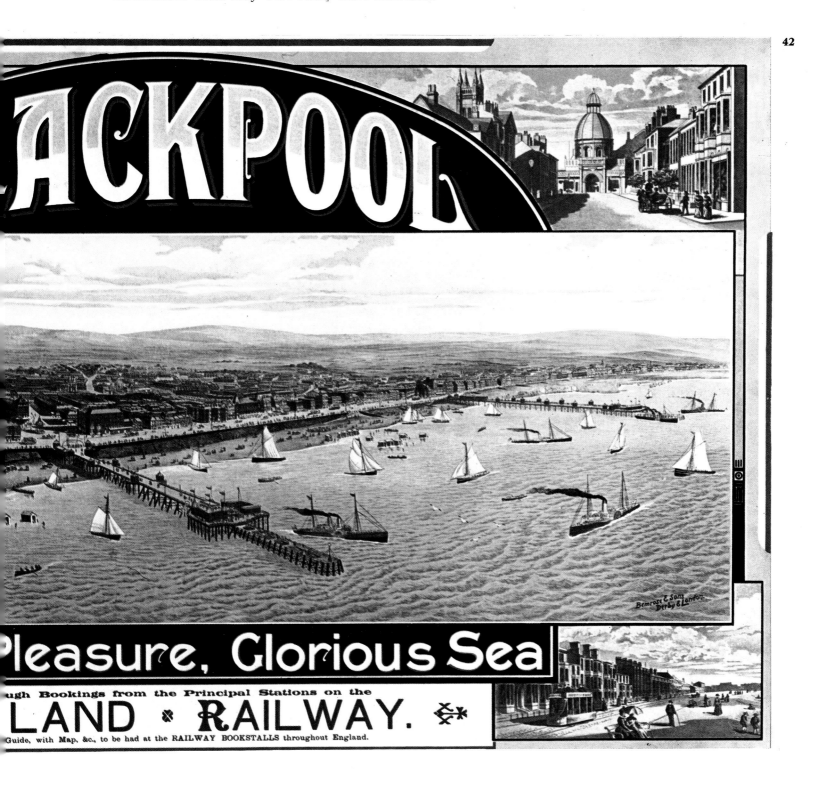

42

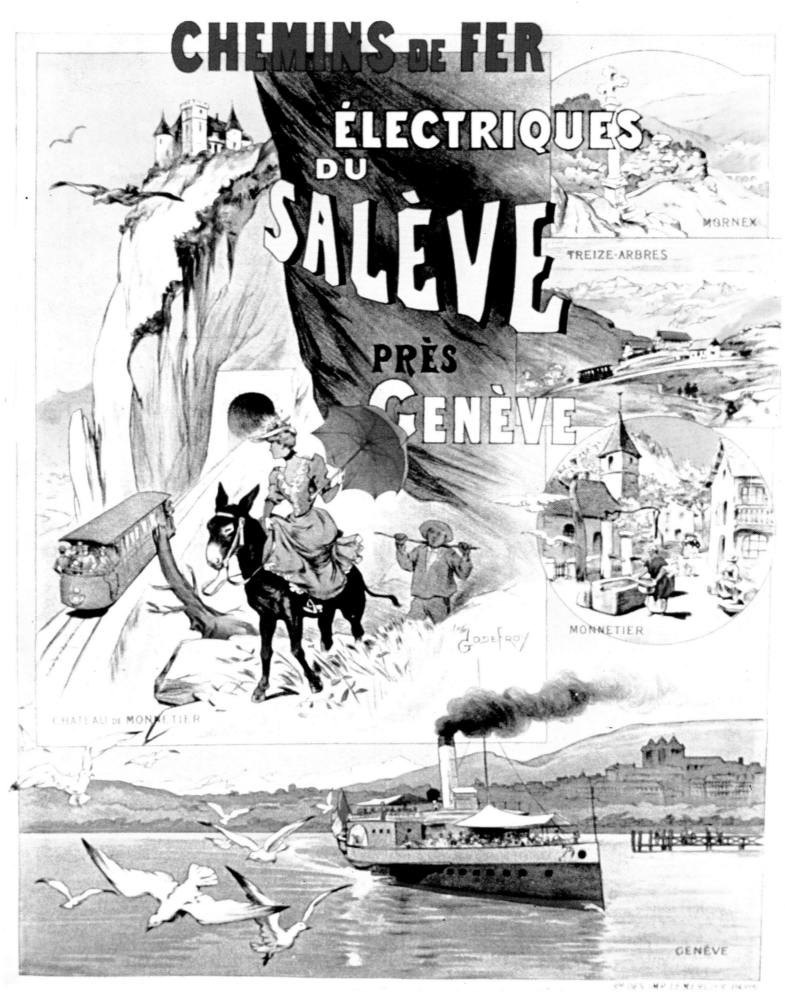

43 Composite view of Salève and Lake Geneva, showing the lake steamers and electric tramway and signed L-G Godefroy.
La Vie du Rail

44 Boulogne – 'La Plage de l'Entente Cordiale' – was two hours and fifty minutes from Paris and three hours from London. It has continued to enjoy the patronage of cross-Channel trippers. Note the bold outlines and colouring, typical of the best French practice at the turn of the century.
La Vie du Rail

in their pictures, the imagination of the French posterists was called into full play. Gustave Fraipont, one of the few artists doing railway work to receive a mention in W. S. Rogers's seminal *A Book of the Poster* of 1901, got round this problem particularly well as his 'Excursions à la Mer' for the Nord company. Details of trains, fares and locations served were placed on three tablets; around these grew art nouveau thistles, their harsh outlines softened by the elegantly drawn wings of a flock of sea-birds which blended with the soft colours and form of the overall design. In the middle ground sat two fashionably dressed ladies, obviously of a more respectable type than the gay young thing in the PLM poster mentioned earlier, and absolutely typical of the sort of female used in the more product-oriented posters of the period.

Less successful (perhaps because it was out of the artist's hands) was the marriage between picture and type in F. Desportes's 1899 poster for the mineral waters at Martigny-les-Bains, reachable by Chemins de Fer d'Orléans et de l'Est. The details of travelling times seemed to have been tacked on as an afterthought to what was otherwise a pleasing, though somewhat formal, design. The exposure of legs here would have been quite acceptable to all tastes, since the model was of classical origin; drawn from the orthodox art of the salons, this type of figure was already very much on the way out by the end of the century. The uncensored opportunities for nudity which the classical figure offered unopposed, were replaced first by a saucier, more popular type of figure and then, in the early years of the twentieth century, by a brief craze for girls in folkloric costume often of dubious derivation and accuracy.

The use of female figures to lure prospective passengers on to trains bound for the coast seems to have been much more of a French preoccupation than it was with the British. At the close of Victoria's reign it would seem, from railway advertising at least, that good healthy open-air pursuits, rather than sexual titillation, were the prerequisites of the *pater familias* in deciding where the family should spend the holidays. Sex seemed to end at the Channel, and a good indication of the contrasting styles of the two countries can be found in a Nord poster for Boulogne from around 1898, during one of the periodic bursts of *entente cordiale* between France and Britain. Depicted in a very French style of bold outlines and strong, broad colour bands, John Bull and a buxom French girl strolled arm-in-arm along the sea shore, two hours and fifty minutes from Paris, and only three hours from London. Boulogne is even 'la Plage de l'Entente Cordiale'! The girl was attired in fashionably long, sweeping clothes, her bosom emphasised by a bold red bodice. J. Bull, on the other hand, harked back to some mythic era of

45-7 In comparison with the gay social world often seen in French seaside posters, the British railway companies went in much more for healthy open-air pursuits for the family. These posters from the North Eastern and Great Western Railways were current in the early years of the twentieth century.
Derek Brough collection (Ian Krause)

quasi-Dickensian joviality; a healthy glow suffused his cheeks, and he wore riding boots and carried a crop. The two appeared so ill-matched that *entente cordiale* seemed doomed.

The British railway companies went in in a big way for linking seaside holidays with vigorous family activity. At the same time as the Nord was promising frolics with the natives, the North Eastern Railway recommended donkey rides on the sands of the Yorkshire coast for the children, whilst nearby, father, in Norfolk jacket and tweeds, could enjoy the advantages of 'The Golfer's Elysium'. By taking the Great Western Railway to North Wales, father could don his plus-fours and be rowed out on to Bala Lake, there to delight in the facilities for free fishing. Usually there tended to be no mention of what mother could do, although she might have been secretly attracted by the handsome Celtic warrior who guarded his imposing castle perched high on the cliffs of the 'Cambrian Coast' poster for the GWR.

The good-clean-holiday-fun type of seaside poster reached its apotheosis in the famous 'Skegness' posters of 1908 *et seq* by John Hassall, issued by the Great Northern Railway. Of the big three English poster designers of the late nineteenth and early twentieth centuries – Dudley Hardy, Hassall and the Beggerstaff Brothers (William Nicholson and James Pryde) – only Hassall did railway work. Though he produced some excellent designs for Frank Pick at London Transport, his fame rests principally with the jolly fisherman of Skegness, arguably the most famous railway poster of all time and one which proved so popular that it continued to be used by the Great Northern and later the London and North Eastern Railway right up until the end of the thirties. It was even reissued in 1968 by way of an anniversary celebration. Hassall's style – rumbustuous, lugubrious and slightly vulgar in an asexual way – had achieved considerable fame for the artist via a long series of posters for such products as Colman's Mustard, Veritas Mantles and Nestlé's Chocolate, and it was an approach that was ideally suited to holiday advertising for the railway. Much of the man went into his work – Bruce Bairnfather's World War I veteran 'Ole Bill' ('If you knows of a better 'ole, go to it') is said to have been modelled on Hassall – and his bright and breezy work formed a marvellous antidote to the decadence and narcissism of the contemporary Beardsley school, who not surprisingly were limited commercially to more esoteric themes.

Hassall was born in Walmer in 1868 and after failing the entrance examinations for Sandhurst, where the British Army trains its officers, he set sail for Manitoba and the farming life. Some success as a kind of homespun artist greeted him there, but it was the publication of some very Christmassy drawings

48 The classic British seaside poster, and one of the most famous railway posters of all time, was John Hassall's 'Skegness is so Bracing'. This is the original Great Northern Railway version, introduced in 1908.
Derek Brough collection (Ian Krause)

49 A further variant on the theme which appeared *circa* 1911.
Derek Brough collection (Ian Krause)

50 Hassall's jolly fisherman continued to adorn the hoardings until well into LNER days. Note the discreet cropping of the picture and the addition of a pier in this later LNER version.
British Transport Museum (B Sharpe)

of his in the *Daily Graphic* in 1890 which really started him on his artistic career. He went to Antwerp to study under van Havemaet, with a short spell spent at art schools in Paris, where he came under the watchful eye of Bouguereau, who was, of course, the first mentor of Chéret and many other classic French posterists. By 1894 *Punch* as well as the *Daily Graphic* was publishing his work, and he succeeded in having a number of his paintings accepted by the Royal Academy. At this stage he contacted David Allen and Sons, a colour-printing firm with an important clientele for poster designs who were then looking out for new artists. They quickly established a sound commercial relationship, lasting for seven years, during which time Hassall gave them several hundred poster designs and achieved for himself a premier reputation as a posterist.

The famous jolly fisherman first came out in 1908. Its design 'had something to do with Romulus and Remus jumping over the little walls of Rome, and Skegness with its glorious air and sands making people jump without anything to jump over', Hassall was to explain many years later. The design (for which, as has been remarked, he received the princely sum of £12) met with such approval from the municipal authorities in Skegness that they later erected statues of the jolly fisherman, incorporated him into the mayoral chain of office and, on Hassall's death in 1948, sent a wreath woven in the form of the leaping figure, a curious case of the recognition of popular culture by an official one. He was, incidentally, accorded the honour of an obituary in *The Times*.

When the London and North Eastern Railway took over the poster, the bold simplicity of the design was emphasised still further by some judicious trimming around the edges, giving the fisherman the appearance of literally leaping out of the frame. By this time, too, the town and the poster had acquired a pier, and the design had sufficient popular appeal for the lettering to be reduced to the absolute minimum. It was an enormously successful design from the first, and Skegness wanted more, so another similar design, featuring a Widow Twankey type of figure skipping gaily along the sands, was produced a year or two later. Many other designers were influenced by it; on the railway side Tony Sarg, an American artist working in Britain, had a London Underground poster for 'Flying at Hendon' dated 1914 which has a noticeable Hassall atmosphere, and in the same year the bustle of Victoria station was conveyed very humorously in a poster for the London Brighton and South Coast Railway. In the 1930s Frank Newbould paid indirect tribute to Hassall's ability to capture character in the very fine 'East Coast Types' series for the London and North Eastern Railway, which recalled many old Hassall models.

Not all railway companies were able to find a surrogate for Hassall, however, and many of them contented themselves with the scenic-view type of poster, assuming that they had a strong holiday or tourist area within their boundaries which they could promote. A wide variety of styles and approaches were used, with purely representational art, often favouring a composite view, in the ascendancy. The opening of the Canadian Pacific route from the east through the Rockies to Vancouver in 1887 was one of the great triumphs of nineteenth-century railroading in North America and it was seized upon by the railway's publicity team for poster ideas. The journey, lasting several days, provided a holiday in itself, as well as bringing the citizens of Toronto and Montreal out to the Great Lakes and the mountains. The Furness Railway in England, a small company whose great crowd-puller was the Lake District, so beloved by Romantic poets and landscape artists, did not produce many posters in the early years of the twentieth century, but those that it did issue were of a very high standard indeed. Some of them, attributed to S. Grant Rowe, featured a curiously Magritte-like approach, where the painting of the landscape centres around another artist figure who is also painting the same landscape; in one design the artist's canvas has been transformed into a system map of the Furness. The Midland Railway's route to Scotland passed through some outstanding scenery in the Peak District and the Pennines which

51

53 Despite the exciting possibilities opened up by the great French posterists and English artists like John Hassall, many railway companies remained conservative in their attitude to poster design. Nevertheless, this Highland Railway poster of 1905 is a splendid example of orthodox Edwardian graphic art.
Derek Brough collection (Ian Krause)

was heavily commended to travellers. Unlike the somewhat impoverished Furness, whose carriage seats, according to Hamilton Ellis in *The Trains We Loved*, 'had been designed for persons of enormous development as to the back, but with thighs so short as to need a perch rather than a seat', the Midland could well afford to, and did, stress the luxurious nature of its carriage accommodation in its advertising. The North Eastern Railway was fortunate in being able to number Frank Pick, later to achieve an enviable reputation as the man behind London Transport's public face, as one of its staff and produced a very fine intensive promotion of its own particular areas, the Yorkshire Dales and the northeast coast.

The Great Western Railway had been one of the first in the field when it came to promoting places along the route as a suitable destination for a daytrip or a full holiday. A poster for Ascot Races dated 1897 is generally accepted as being GWR's first pictorial piece, but the faults endemic in this design – cluttered layout, too much information and an overbusy illustration – were never really eradicated in its later output. Besides being able to offer travel to Ireland via the railway-developed port of Fishguard, the GWR was very keen to promote Devon and Cornwall as holiday centres. Its usual artist in the years around 1908 was Alec Fraser, a capable and immediately recognisable painter but one who suffered from a rather remorseless use of greens and browns, which gave the company's posters an unpleasantly dense, impenetrable appearance.

54 A naive but delightful turn-of-the-century poster from the Mersey Railway. The design of the cars owed much to American influence, and the lavish interiors contrast strongly with today's spartan commuter accommodation. *British Transport Museum (B Sharpe)*

55-58 Four scenic-view type posters put out by the Furness Railway *circa* 1905. They are probably the work of S Grant Rowe, RSA. *Derek Brough collection (Ian Krause)*

NORTH EASTERN RAILWAY.

THE Yorkshire Coast

Breezy—Bracing.

FOR PARTICULARS WITH REFERENCE TO TRAIN SERVICE & CHEAP TICKETS TO THE YORKSHIRE COAST WRITE THE CHIEF PASSENGER AGENT. DEPARTMENT A. NORTH EASTERN RAILWAY. YORK.

59

YORKSHIRE'S ENCHANTING DALES

"EVER CHARMING, EVER NEW,
WHEN WILL THE LANDSCAPE TIRE THE VIEW?"

NIDDERDALE. RYEDALE. SWALEDALE.
TEESDALE. WENSLEYDALE. WHARFEDALE.
FOR FULL INFORMATION WRITE THE CHIEF PASSENGER AGENT,
DEPARTMENT A, NORTH EASTERN RAILWAY YORK.

NORTHUMBRIA.

THE LAND OF CASTLES.
AN UNEXPLORED GROUND
FOR TOURISTS, WITH
MAGNIFICENT COAST &
INLAND SCENERY & INTERESTING
RUINS OF THE ROMAN WALL.
Particulars as to Trains, Fares, &c. can be
obtained on application to the Chief Passenger
Agent, Dept A, North Eastern Railway, York.

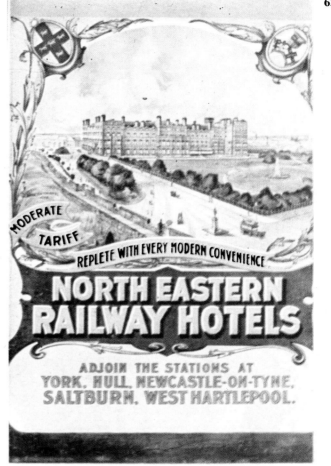

MODERATE TARIFF

REPLETE WITH EVERY MODERN CONVENIENCE

NORTH EASTERN RAILWAY HOTELS

ADJOIN THE STATIONS AT
YORK. HULL. NEWCASTLE-ON-TYNE.
SALTBURN. WEST HARTLEPOOL.

North Eastern Railway

YORKSHIRE COAST

FOR PARTICULARS WITH REFERENCE TO TRAIN
SERVICE & CHEAP TICKETS TO THE YORKSHIRE
COAST WRITE THE CHIEF PASSENGER AGENT
DEPT A. NORTH EASTERN RAILWAY, YORK.

NORTH EASTERN RAILWAY.

HISTORIC YORK

THE THRESHOLD OF
ENGLANDS BEST
HOLIDAY GROUND

CIRCULAR
TOURS AND
CHEAP TICKETS
IN ALL DIRECTIONS

EXPERIENCED GUIDES to the **CITY of YORK** can be arranged
for by communicating with the CHIEF PASSENGER AGENT, DEPT A. NORTH EASTERN
RAILWAY. YORK.

NORTH EASTERN RAILWAY
SUMMER HOLIDAYS
NORTH EAST ENGLAND

FOR FURTHER PARTICULARS WRITE THE CHIEF PASSENGER AGENT DEPARTMENT A. NORTH EASTERN RAILWAY. YORK.

THE YORKSHIRE COAST

"To those who know thee no words can paint
And those who know thee know all words are faint."
RAILWAY STATIONS WITHIN EASY REACH. FOR PARTICULARS WRITE THE
CHIEF PASSENGER AGENT, DEPARTMENT A, NORTH EASTERN RAILWAY YORK.

59-69 Some of the best posters from the Edwardian period were put out by the North Eastern Railway, with whom Frank Pick, later to achieve considerable fame with London Transport, was a member of staff. Its promotion of the north east coast and the Yorkshire Dales as holiday areas was especially vigorous. Note the advertising of the company's hotel facilities; Edwardian railway activities covered many fields.
Derek Brough collection (Ian Krause)

NORTH EASTERN ENGLAND
The Land of Lore & Legend.

for full particulars apply
Chief Passenger Agent, Department A.
NORTH EASTERN RAILWAY, YORK.

NORTH EASTERN RAILWAY

TRANQUIL
SOLITUDE

THE
YORKSHIRE MOORS

WRITE THE CHIEF PASSENGER AGENT. ADVERTISING DEPARTMENT.
NORTH EASTERN RAILWAY. YORK. FOR PARTICULARS.

70 Pages from the July 1913 issue of *Railway and Travel Monthly*, showing the summer season's new railway posters. Note, in addition to the Great Western Railway's famous 'Holiday Haunts' series of travel booklets and the rare Festiniog poster, the escapist Lancashire and Yorkshire design. Unlike many railways which affected a high-class image, the Lanky made little attempt to play down its essentially working-class patronage in its advertising. Such a poster as this would have had an obvious appeal to northern millworkers.
Derek Brough collection (Ian Krause)

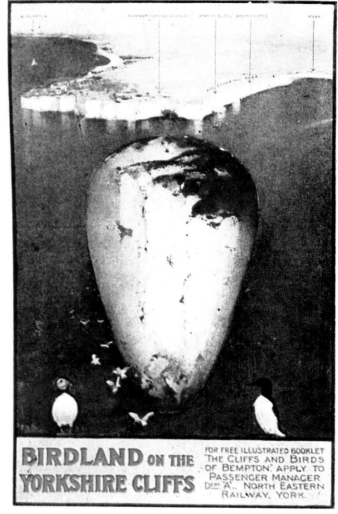

BIRDLAND ON THE YORKSHIRE CLIFFS

FOR FREE ILLUSTRATED BOOKLET 'THE CLIFFS AND BIRDS OF BEMPTON' APPLY TO PASSENGER MANAGER D^{PT} 'A'. NORTH EASTERN RAILWAY, YORK.

70

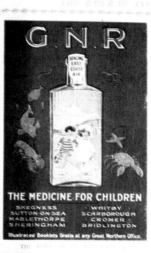

The Best Route

FOR

Comfortable Travel

AND Picturesque Scenery

Midland Railway Holiday Travel Series

HARROGATE, ILKLEY, GRASSINGTON, AND BEN RHYDDING.

The Eden Valley

THE VALLEY OF THE EDEN

APPLEBY CASTLE, ON THE EDEN

THE EDEN AT ARMATHWAITE

EN ROUTE TO SCOTLAND

71-75 Pre-grouping Midland Railway posters. The Midland was one of the most solid and dependable of the British companies, enjoying a considerable share of the traffic between London and Scotland through the highly scenic Pennine hills.
Derek Brough collection (Ian Krause)

76 North British Railway poster of the late Edwardian period showing the Forth Bridge.
Vic Goldberg collection (Malcolm Malins)

77 A novel way of promoting the Ayrshire coast holiday resorts served by the Glasgow and South Western Railway. Again, note the emphasis on healthy open-air pursuits.
British Transport Museum (B Sharpe)

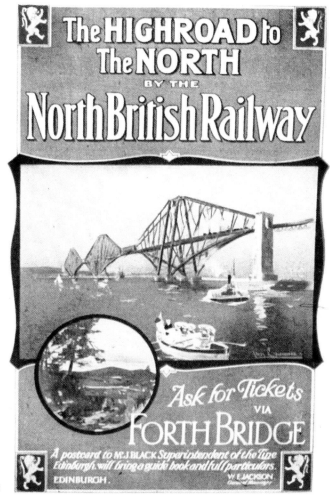

THE DELIGHTFUL DISTRICTS
HERE AND THERE AND
EVERYWHERE SERVED BY

THE CALEDONIAN RAILWAY ARE
RAPIDLY REACHED BY THE
UNIQUELY COMFORTABLE
EXPRESS TRAINS, WHICH

LEAD FAR AND NEAR
IN QUARTERS BEST.
NORTH AND SOUTH AND
EAST AND WEST

TRUE
TO
TIME

LANCASHIRE & YORKSHIRE RLY.
THE BUSINESS LINE

COMFORTABLE TRAVEL
BY
EXPRESS TRAINS

VICTORIA STATION MANCHESTER

THE MOST CONVENIENT STARTING POINT FOR ALL PARTS.

LUXURIOUS VESTIBULED
LAVATORY CARRIAGES

THROUGH SERVICES
DINING CAR TRAINS

Train and Boat Connections with the Principal Business Centres and Pleasure Resorts in

ENGLAND, IRELAND, SCOTLAND & WALES

For full particulars of Fares, Train Services, &c., apply to the JOHN A. F ASPINALL, GENERAL MANAGER
Passenger Superintendent, Victoria Station, Manchester.

78 An unusual acrostic poster from the Caledonian Railway. Some idea of the intense pride of the company can be gained from this design, which featured their famous *Cardean* locomotive.
Vic Goldberg collection (Malcolm Malins)

79 As well as its working-class clientele, the Lancashire and Yorkshire enjoyed considerable patronage from the business traffic in its area. For this it provided modern and efficient, if somewhat utilitarian, facilities, and this was emphasised in its advertising. This poster of 1909 stresses the improved quality of its equipment over the years.
Derek Brough collection (Ian Krause)

80 The London and North Western Railway also prided itself on the efficiency and frequency of its train services between Birmingham and London. This poster offers a novel way of interpreting factual information on train departures in a visual manner.
Derek Brough collection (Ian Krause)

81 The London and North Western Railway had the foresight to employ the famous marine artist and Fellow of the Royal Academy Norman Wilkinson to design its posters for the Holyhead-Ireland steamer services. Such work as this played an important role in taking art out of the galleries and into the public eye. Wilkinson was later to superintend the influential range of posters commissioned by the London, Midland and Scottish Railway from eminent Academicians.
Derek Brough collection (Ian Krause)

82 The North Western's lead in the use of recognised artists was soon taken up by other railway companies. This Midland Railway poster of *circa* 1910 advertised steamer services between the railway port of Heysham and Douglas, Isle of Man.
Derek Brough collection (Ian Krause)

Along with a number of other railways, the Great Western had a craze in the Edwardian period for producing figures in folkloric national costume in their poster designs. Its 'See Your Own Country First' poster, a fine visual pun, featured cunningly juxtapositioned maps of Cornwall and Italy, between which it was suggested 'there is a great similarity . . . in shape, climate and natural beauties.' The natural beauties were two girls in 'authentic' peasant costume from each country, an English rose and a sultry Mediterranean maiden. Less rampantly nationalistic was a Belgian poster for the Ostend–Dover ferry, where a beautifully painted group of figures in typically Belgian costume awaited the arrival of the cross-channel ferry. The North Eastern Railway had a very good poster with the clear, Hassall-like outline of a Dutch woman in traditional costume against a simple background. Inevitably this had a windmill, but, like all good posters, this advertisement for the Hull–Rotterdam service gave people the image of foreign travel they wanted in an unpretentious and pleasant way.

Since international boundaries had been breached by the coming of the railway and the establishment of complementary shipping services, foreign travel had quite a substantial role to play in Edwardian railway advertising. As early as 1893, the Canadian Pacific had produced an astonishing poster, composed of outlandishly grotesque parodies of a wide range of silly foreigners and social archetypes. Besides the usual details of internal fares to places like Banff, Winnipeg and Halifax, a Ned Kelly figure carried a sandwich-board proclaiming a return

fare to Australia of $401 and a bearded patriarch advertised round-the-world trips for $610. Usually, however, international travel was advertised in a far more diplomatic manner. It was quite a common practice for the railways of one country to advertise

extensively in another, with a poster solely for export use and not employed domestically. Examples of this were an Egyptian State Railways poster for the pyramids used in France, or an Iraqi State Railways poster with the English tourist market very much in mind, right down to the genteelly worded 'A glorious interlude for those travelling to and from Europe, Iran and the East.' Another common practice was to take a domestic poster and translate the copy into the appropriate language for use abroad. A splendid illustration of this was the poster commissioned from the great Milanese poster house of Ricordi to commemorate the Simplon tunnel, $12\frac{1}{2}$ miles in length, begun in 1898 and completed in 1906. An exhibition was held in Milan to

83 This Canadian Pacific (Eastern Division) poster makes use of photo-based city views. The composite approach was very popular in the pre-World War I years, but such graphic anarchy as this was the exception rather than the rule.
CP Rail

84 London and North Western Railway poster of 1909 contrasting the speeding two-hour express of that year with the Roman foot soldiers of 50 BC.
Derek Brough collection (Ian Krause)

85 Posters issued by the railway companies of one country were frequently used (suitably translated) in another. This Belgian poster of 1913 for the Dover-Ostend ferry service is the same basic design as that shown in Fig 3 in its English version.
La Vie du Rail

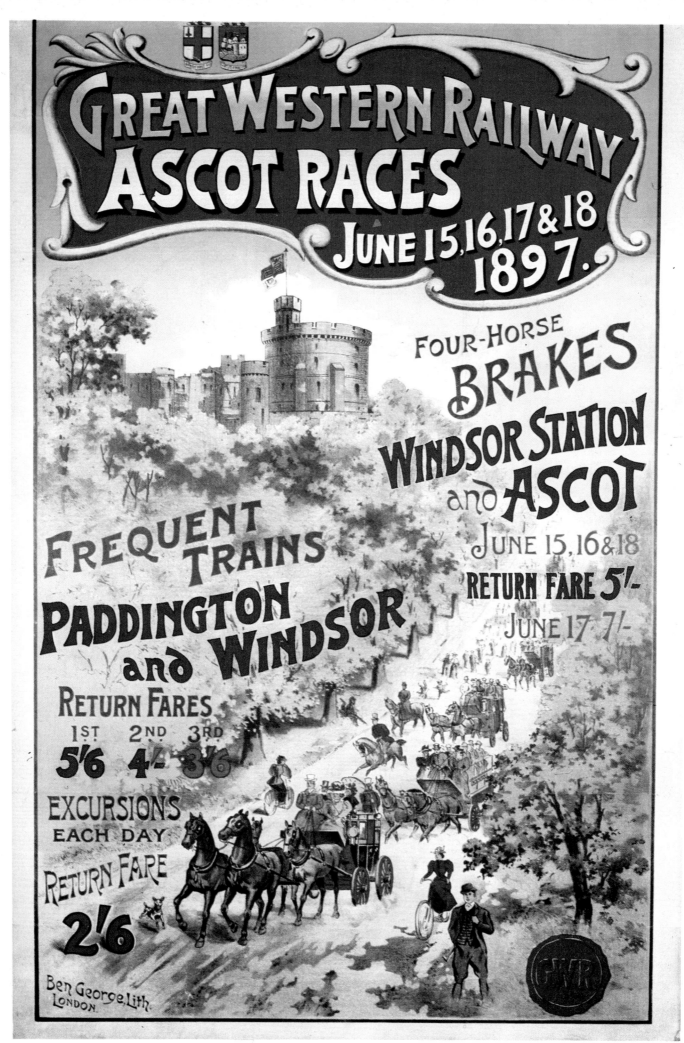

86 One of the Great Western's very first pictorial posters, advertising the Ascot race meeting of June 1897. Such a barrage of typographical and visual information was typical of the early days of pictorial advertising.
Great Western Railway Museum, Swindon (Ian Krause)

87 An unusually delicate GWR poster from the turn of the century. St Michael's Mount was to figure prominently in GWR advertising for many years to come. *Great Western Railway Museum, Swindon (Ian Krause)*

90

88 Christmas excursions in the Edwardian era, Great Western style.
Derek Brough collection (Ian Krause)

89 The beginnings of the GWR's 'Cornish Riviera' advertising campaign, *circa* 1908.
Derek Brough collection (Ian Krause)

90 A much more vigorous GWR design, promoting the alternative holiday areas served by the company in North Wales.
Great Western Railway Museum, Swindon (Ian Krause)

91 The early GWR posters were normally unsigned, but some of these posters are very probably the work of Alec Fraser. Note the mention of motor services, a common ancillary service operated by railways in pre-World War I days.
Derek Brough collection (Ian Krause)

92 The GWR also acquired a considerable share of the Irish sea trade, opening up the lakes of Southern Ireland to English visitors.
Derek Brough collection (Ian Krause)

93 An unusual Great Western poster advertising the company's dining car services.
Derek Brough collection (Ian Krause)

94 An example from the brief craze for folkloric costume posters, issued by the North Eastern Railway around 1910 for its Hull-Rotterdam sailings.
Derek Brough collection

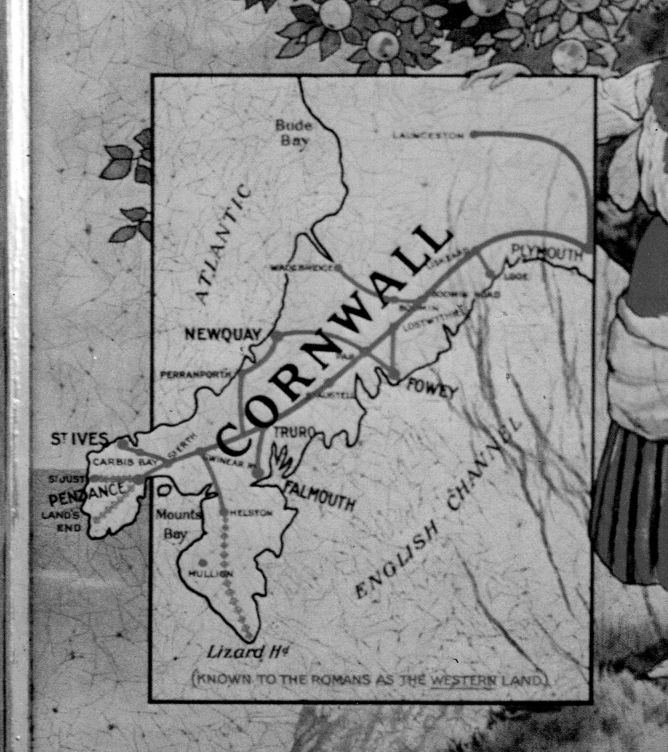

GREAT WEST
SEE YOUR OWN

CORNWALL

THERE IS A GREAT SIMILARITY B
CORNWALL
IN SHA

(COPYRIGHT DESIGN)

FRANK POTTER. GENERAL MANAGER.

ERN RAILWAY
COUNTRY FIRST

MILAN   VENICE

BOLOGNA

GENOA

FLORENCE

LEGHORN

ADRIATIC

ITALY

ANCONA

ROME

MEDITERRANEAN

NAPLES   BRINDISI

Gulf
of
Taranto

Cape S.ta Maria di Leuca

REGGIO

Cape Spartivento

(KNOWN TO THE GREEKS AS THE WESTERN LAND.)

ETWEEN
AND ITALY
PE, CLIMATE & NATURAL BEAUTIES.

celebrate this considerable feat and Leopoldo M. Metlicoviz's poster for this event was printed in several languages and widely distributed around Europe. It was a strongly allegorical design, one of the most dramatic railway posters ever produced. The blinding light of the sun as the train left the tunnel silhouetted the mysterious figures on the front of the locomotive, partially illuminated from behind by the engine's fire, to produce a most striking contrast.

This was one of the few posters issued in the pre-World War I period in which the actual train or railway played any significant visual part. Occasionally a landscape view might be broken by the elegant curve of a viaduct (as with the Midland Railway

posters mentioned earlier), but the power and might (and consequent visual qualities) of the steam locomotive were not generally drawn upon by poster artists until the late 1920s. There were a few, though: the London and North Western had a naive but wholly delightful advertisement for its two-hour expresses from Euston to Birmingham, where locomotives were grouped roundhouse-style under clocks which bore the train times, and another where a litho of the Roman road to the north was contrasted with the speeding express of 1909. The Lancashire and Yorkshire ('The Business Line') had a typically dour design for expresses to and from Manchester Victoria featuring one of their very earliest engines and, by way of comparison, one of

96

95 A splendid visual pun used on a GWR poster of 1908. This was one of the very few railway posters known to have been printed on enamel sheet in the popular Edwardian manner of advertising. Paper was the medium normally employed, since the items advertised by railways (cheap fares, excursions, etc) had a shorter selling life than the proprietary goods advertised on enamel signs.
British Transport Museum (B Sharpe)

96 This Iraqi State Railways was probably designed and executed in Britain under commission, since it is hard to believe the native country could present itself in such a clichéd image, with caravan, hookah and shifty-eyed bedouins.
La Vie du Rail

97 Egyptian State Railways poster of 1911 as used in France.
La Vie du Rail

the latest. The prestigious 'Southern Belle' express of the London, Brighton and South Coast Railway was frozen in full stride on a 1908 poster while the departure times were given underneath. The moment of emergence from the Simplon tunnel was used once again by the Chemins de Fer Jura-Simplon. This latter poster as it is illustrated here is a good example of the habit of printing up part of a run of posters without the lettering, so that they could be placed in store ready for use at a later date when a new promotion was urgently required. The new lettering could then be rapidly printed on and the finished poster on display far quicker than if new colour blocks for the lithograph had to be originated.

As Attilio Rossi has observed in *I Manifesti*, the travel poster has to allude to such things as the speed and punctuality of services, the convenience of dining car facilities on the train and the luxurious appointments of hotels as well as publicising the eventual destination, and at the same time it has to make the latter as appealing as possible to give a reason for emphasising the speed and frequency of services. Ancillary services such as shipping connections had also to be covered; the Midland, Caledonian and Great Western companies rapidly followed the London and North Western's initiative of using Norman Wilkinson's seascapes with the very minimum of wording – just the company's name and some simple phrase like 'Dublin and Holyhead'. Freight services were not advertised to any great

extent in the pre-war era since the railways enjoyed an almost complete monopoly of this traffic.

In view of the diversifying activities in poster advertising, and the increasing quality of the work, it was high time that attention was paid to the actual display of posters. The frontispiece to *A History of Advertising*, published in the mid-Victorian period, showed a railway station of 1874 in which barely a square foot of usable wall space is not bedecked with advertisements for Lamplough's Pyretic Saline, Crosby's Cough Elixir, Holloway's Ointment, Thurston's Billiard Tables, Goodall's Yorkshire Relish

98 One of the best of all the international posters from the pre-World War I years. This allegorical poster for the commemorative exhibition in Milan following the opening of the Simplon tunnel in 1906 came from the great poster-producing firm of Ricordi and was designed by Leopoldo M Metlicovitz, the head of one of Ricordi's printing departments. It was printed in most of the European languages and was widely distributed.
La Vie du Rail

99 Poster, featuring a painting by Secrétan, for the London, Brighton and South Coast Railway's prestigious 'Southern Belle' express *circa* 1914. This train, introduced in 1908, was the forerunner of a long line of luxury commuter trains between Brighton and Victoria, which came to an end with the withdrawal of the 'Brighton Belle' in 1972.
Derek Brough collection (Ian Krause)

99

and the like. By the turn of the century the situation had become so chaotic that one District Railway traveller complained that it was difficult to decide 'whether one was at Victoria, Virol or Vinolia.' A trade advertising agent of the North Eastern Railway put forward a scheme in 1911 whereby station sites should be neatly divided into numbered spaces for commercial advertising and for the posters issued by the railway company so there should be no clash. This sensible plan was widely adopted by major railway companies and advertisers.

In the same period, London's Underground, under the guiding hand of Frank Pick, established precedents in the whole field of the railway's public face which are still being widely followed. Pick was born in Stamford, Lincolnshire, in 1878, the son of a draper, trained as a solicitor and, as has already been mentioned, cut his teeth in railway work with the North Eastern. He came to London Underground Railways, as it then was, in 1906, rose to be managing director and at the time of his death in 1941 he had become the Vice-Chairman of London Transport. The move south offered Pick a much broader field of possibilities than had hitherto been open to him, and he used his opportunities to the full. He was a close friend of A. S. Hartrick from the Central School of Arts and Crafts in London, a college which boasted a highly advanced approach not just to advertising work, but to the whole field of industrial design and public relations as well. He chose to commission posters almost exclusively from established artists like Hassall, Fred Taylor, Sir Frank Brangwyn and Mabel Lucie Attwell and his later stable included such illustrious names as Rex Whistler, E. McKnight Kauffer, Edward Wadsworth, Graham Sutherland, Sir Jacob Epstein and Henry Moore; the combination of aesthetic quality, popular interest and commercial effectiveness was from the very start a winning one.

He also made the first serious approach ever made by a transport organisation to the co-ordination of design. Window-dressing was what it amounted to, but it meant, for instance, that station architecture (in the capable hands of Charles Holden) should relate from one station to the next, but that variety should exist between the stations in one district or on a particular stretch of line and those in another. The smallest detail should be of vital importance; the design of a station seat was as worthy of care and attention as the design of a whole train unit, the pattern of a wall-tile (he usually had Harold Stabler do the little details like this) must be relevant to the overall furnishing of a station. The posters were the most memorable feature of the new image.

Beginning with the quintessentially Edwardian designs of John Hassall, Pick and his artists rapidly evolved a style which was to place the railway poster firmly in the twentieth century. A Hassall poster of 1908 showed a confused couple up from the country approaching a superbly rotund policeman in an underground booking-hall for directions. With a brilliant common touch, Hassall's genial copper gestured with his thumb towards the easy-to-read

101

tube map on the wall behind. 'No need to ask a p'liceman' was the reassuring message, backed up by an unobtrusive 'Underground to Anywhere/Quickest Way, Cheapest Fare'. Within months a much more revolutionary approach had come to stay; since the artist selected was invariably an established one, he could be relied on to see his subject in his own special way, and thus to offer the viewer new ways of looking at old favourites like Epping Forest or Kew Gardens. The Fred Taylor 'Sunday Concerts' poster of 1912, for instance, took the listener up into the balcony to look down on the flower-strewn stage. Once the appetite had been whetted, the potential traveller was told exactly how to reach his destination: to 'Book to Hampstead or Golders

100 Fred Taylor's 'Sunday Concerts' poster of 1912, one of the best of the early Underground posters. Such posters as this were to set the pace in railway advertising for the next quarter of a century.
British Transport Museum (B Sharpe)

101 In this view of Malton station on the North Eastern Railway, the company's notice boards seem rather lost in the welter of advertisements for Van Houten's Cocoa, Stephens' Ink and Mazawatee Tea. Nevertheless, the railway company has clearly appropriated the prime eye-level sites for itself. Regulations were introduced in 1911 detailing the location of railway and private advertising on railway premises.
Arnold Wood collection

102 Earl's Court station on London's Underground network in 1910. The prominent siting of maps and posters can be clearly seen.
Arnold Wood collection

103 A much more orderly system of advertising at Haworth on the Midland Railway, with the company's posters on the station walls and commercial enamel signs on the platform fencing. This station is still in use today, on the steam-worked Keighley and Worth Valley Railway in Yorkshire.
Arnold Wood collection

102

103

Green' for Hampstead Fair, or to go 'By Tram to Kew Bridge' for the spring flowers in Kew Gardens. Because it had no competition and thus was free from the hard sell, the London Transport poster could afford to be amiable and pleasing. One of the most charming was a 1913 Mabel Lucie Attwell sketch of two little children greeting a rabbit in a country area served by the District Railway – 'Hello, did you come by Underground?'

Such idylls were rudely shattered by the onset of the Great War. The production of colourful travel posters ceased overnight, though Pick did succeed in commissioning Edward Johnston in 1915 to design a new *sans serif* fount – the famous 'underground letter' still is in use today. Mabel Lucie Attwell's children were replaced on the hoardings by civilians fleeing their burning homes. 'To arms, citizens of the empire' an army officer urged them. On Union Pacific billboards an ammunition train screamed through the night towards a devilish German foe, the old familiar elk replaced by the American eagle beneath whose outspread wings Woodrow Wilson cried 'The world must be made safe for democracy!' In Germany, Field Marshal von Hindenburg through a poster by Schauroth expressed his thanks to the citizens of Stuttgart for providing a hospital train – a *Lazarettzug* – for the Eastern Front. The world would not be the same again.

104 A novel advertising gimmick from the early days of the London and North Eastern Railway. It is debatable whether the engines actually ran sporting these excursion handbills, or if this was merely a posed publicity photograph.
Arnold Wood collection (LPC)

105 An aggressive World War I poster put out by the Union Pacific, emphasising the important part railways played in the war effort.
Union Pacific Railroad Museum collection

106 This Jura-Simplon Railway poster of *circa* 1900 demonstrates the occasional practice of printing up posters minus the lettering, which could then be added at a later date, either handwritten or printed. This was a convenient way of getting new information on to the noticeboards without the time and expense involved in creating a fresh design.
La Vie du Rail

"The world must

be made safe for Democracy!"
— WOODROW WILSON —

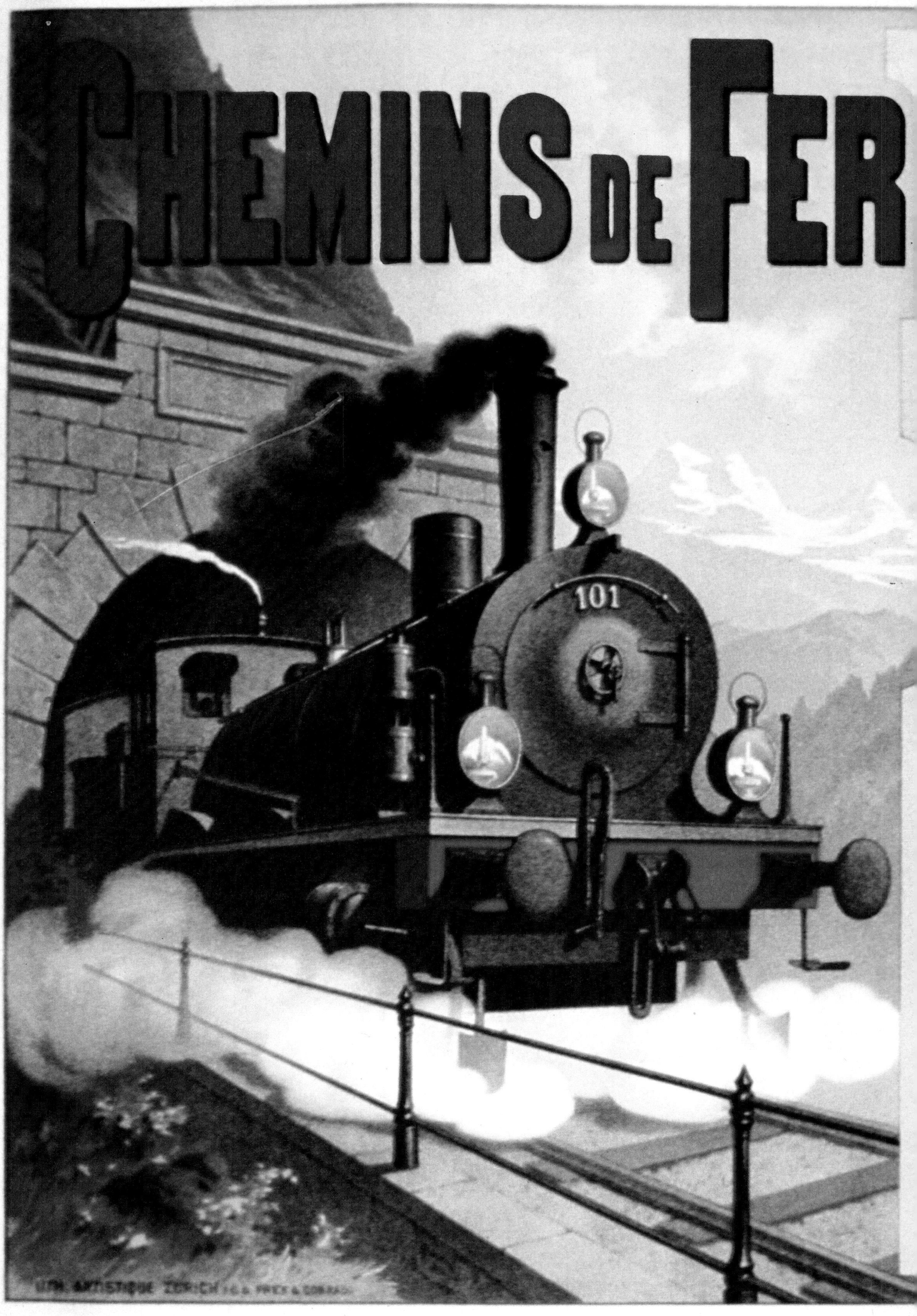
CHEMINS DE FER
101

JURA-SIMPLON

Chapter Three

Beside the Seaside, Beside the Sea...

It took a long time for the railways in the belligerent countries to recover from the effects of World War I. Track, worn down by the constant heavy traffic of supply trains or destroyed by enemy action, had to be replaced and repaired. Locomotives and stock, pushed far beyond their normal limits of endurance, had to be overhauled, shelled-out stations rebuilt. Little cash or energy could be spared for such secondary matters as publicity, and there was a fallow period of some four or five years in the production of railway posters after the cessation of hostilities.

It was very obvious that things were not to be the same again. The cosy world of John Hassall's posters now seemed very far away, and so too did (in the image-makers' eyes) the jolly family holiday by the sea. In 1911 the Union Pacific had undertaken an advertising campaign based around the slogan 'California Calls You'. The central figure was a demure girl in *matelot* top carrying a parasol; she sat on a grassy mound and gazed wistfully away from the artist towards distant snow-capped mountains.

107 GWR poster of 1908, carrying Alec Fraser's monogram and showing the characteristic lettering style in use at this period.
British Transport Museum (B Sharpe)

108 Symptomatic of the changed post-war advertising world, the girl in this 1922 Union Pacific design looks confidently at the viewer. In the 1911 version, her legs were hidden by a sailor suit and she gazed shyly away with downcast eyes.
Union Pacific Railroad

108

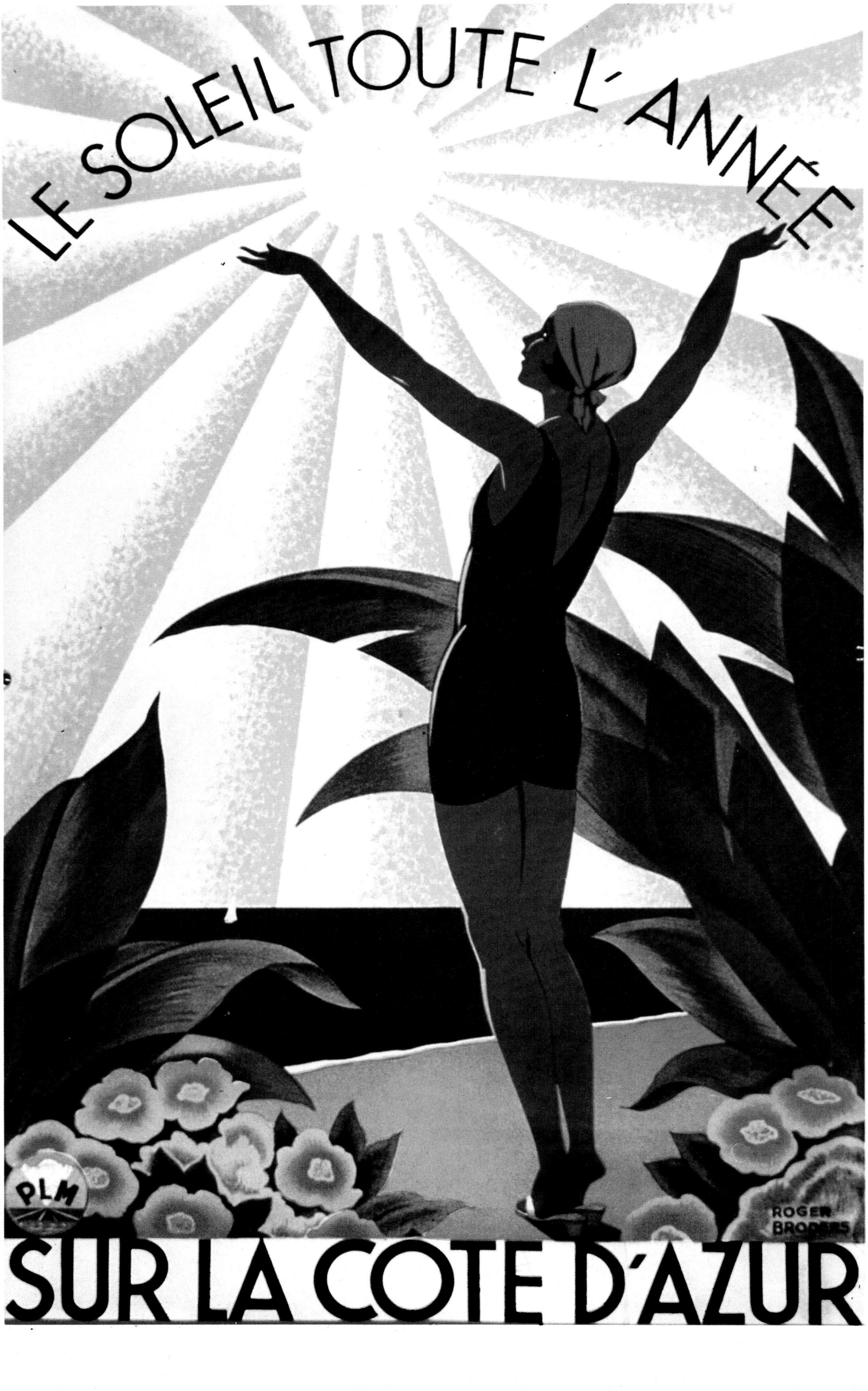
LE SOLEIL TOUTE L'ANNÉE
PLM
ROGER BRODERS
SUR LA COTE D'AZUR

When the advertisement reappeared in 1922 this Maxfield Parrish-style young miss was still sitting on the same flower-strewn bank, but now she stared brazenly at her audience and her skirt had ridden up above her calves. After the bourgeois repression of the Victorian and Edwardian periods, the 'bright young thing' had come to stay. The seaside was no longer the picture-postcard world where kiddies went for donkey rides along the sands or one strolled leisurely along the coast, taking in the castles and rocky cliffs. Now the advertising men's vision was of a place where (in an early London and North Eastern Railway poster) scantily-clad young girls frolicked in the waves proclaiming their emancipation flagrantly from the bows of a rowing boat, whilst gentlemen blew up inflatable water-wings and the donkeys stayed very much in the background. Roger Broders did a poster for the PLM, extolling the Côte d'Azur – where one could enjoy 'Le soleil toute l'année' – through the silhouetted figure of a flapper in bathing suit ecstatically worshipping the sun.

The influence of Frank Pick grew and grew. 'He has mapped out delightful and economical excursions for the working-class family,' wrote Percy Bradshaw in his 1925 book *Art and Advertising*, 'he has robbed the wet Bank Holiday of its former terrors, and he has given imaginative artists a free hand in proving that Art and advertising are inseparable terms.' In the early 1920s Vorticism was very much the driving force behind English artists, and Pick saw to it that it was fully represented on the London Transport hoardings of the day. Epstein and Clive Gardner were among the artists used, and Pick even succeeded in making Edward Wadsworth's enor-

mous and extraordinary painting 'Dazzle Ships' into a poster in 1936. The Vorticist who benefited most from the patronage of Frank Pick was E. McKnight Kauffer, to whom the booking-halls and long winding corridors and platforms of the Underground stations became his own art gallery. Pick had first used Kauffer as early as 1915, employing largely conventional themes and subjects, but it was his 'London History at the London Museum' poster of 1922 which really brought him into the public eye. Kauffer took as his motif the Fire of London, producing a Cubist pattern of reds and yellows in the centre of the poster (large areas were left blank, a final realisation that cramming every possible section of the poster with detail was not the way to successful design). Apart from the caption, the only other lettering was the typically terse directive of 'Dover Street or St James's Park Station.' In 1924, in marked contrast to

109 The Côte d'Azur by Roger Broders for the PLM

---

110 Though some Underground posters gave clear and precise travel instructions, others encouraged traffic by a more subliminal approach. This 1913 poster by Everill Bennett merely presents an image of winter sales, and stimulates travellers to find their own way to their favourite shops. The information required could easily be derived from the maps which Frank Pick was careful to site nearby. *British Transport Museum (B Sharpe)*

---

111 By way of contrast to Bennett's design, this 1930 piece by E McKnight Kauffer is brutally severe in its design and colouring. The poster does not actually advertise anything; this absence of commercial message was a luxury which the Underground's virtual monopoly of traffic enabled it to afford. McKnight Kauffer also did landscape designs for the Great Western Railway in the late 1930s. *British Transport Museum (B Sharpe)*

110

111

Everil Bennett's earlier design for 'Winter Sales', the elegantly windswept figures gave way to a fragmented pattern of rain, umbrellas and planes of colour. Like the Italian Futurists with whom they had close affinities, the Vorticists were fascinated by the stark industrial design of things such as factories, dams and power stations, and Kauffer incorporated this functional interest into his 'Power: the Nerve Centre of London's Underground' of 1930. The clenched fist and sinewy forearm give an uncomfortable foreboding of the political tendencies of the day; a possible influence in its form and colouring was Severo Pozzati's famous 1928 poster for 'Noveltex' collars.

Pick's incentive was taken up by the main-line railways of Britain in the mid-1920s. In 1923 the myriad small and not-so-small railway companies had been brought together to form four major companies: the London, Midland and Scottish Railway, serving the northbound routes in the west, the London and North Eastern Railway going north up

the east coast, the Southern Railway in the south-east and parts of Devon, and the Great Western Railway in the rest of Devon, Cornwall, the south Midlands and Wales. Whilst a strong element of competition remained, particularly on the routes from London to Scotland and London to Birmingham, the frantic scramble for passengers perpetrated by the old companies was changed by the grouping into a more monopolistic situation. Instead of slogan-mongering, the publicity departments could now afford more time and money on good design and pleasing the eye.

Very early in the new company's existence, Norman Wilkinson of the Royal Academy (who had done a number of posters for the London and North Western Railway in earlier days) suggested to the LMS authorities that they commission members of the Academy to design a series of posters for them. Over the years this resulted in some memorable designs by Augustus John, George Clausen, Sir William Orpen, Sir Bertram Mackennal, D. Y.

LMS SPEED
BY SIR BERTRAM MACKENNAL. R.A.

LMS   STIRLING
BY SIR D. Y. CAMERON. R.A.

Cameron and Maurice Greiffenhargen. The latter's 'Carlisle: The Gateway to Scotland' was a design calculated to stir the heart of any red-blooded Englishman. A vividly coloured and meticulously detailed St George, mounted on a charger, stood by one of Carlisle's ancient gateways, through which the high road could be seen passing over a packhorse bridge on its way to the Scottish mountains, seen dimly in the background. This poster (one of the first to use the 'gateway to . . .' approach which was to be done to death in later years) was among the nine original canvases exhibited in London in January 1924, which a few months later were to become a familiar sight on LMS hoardings. Others from this first batch were D. Y. Cameron's 'Scottish Highlands', George Henry's 'Edinburgh Castle', 'Speed' by Sir Bertram Mackennal (a monotone plaque in low relief depicting a winged man in flight) and 'The Permanent Way' by Stanhope Forbes.

The latter made good use of the repeated patterns formed by the tracklaying gang at work and the way their shadows cast the sleepers in relief. No attempt was made to glamourise Tom's gang; they were simply doing their job under the watchful eye of the felt-hatted gaffer on the left of the picture. It was a sympathetic attitude to the working man, with close affinities to the type of poster Hassall had produced some years earlier to protest against pubs closing on Sundays, and this stood in marked contrast to the

112 In contrast to the patronage of exciting young artists encouraged by Frank Pick on London Transport, the London, Midland and Scottish Railway opted for the more orthodox talents of Royal Academicians for a series of posters of which the first appeared in 1924. 'Speed' by Sir Bertram Mackennal was one of this first batch of LMS/ Royal Academy posters.
British Transport Museum (B Sharpe)

113 'Stirling' by DY Cameron.
British Transport Museum (B Sharpe)

LMS   CARL

THE GATEWAY

BY MAURICE GR

ISLE

TO SCOTLAND.

TIFFENHAGEN. R.A.

LMS THE PERMA
RELA

ANENT WAY

AYING

115

116　LMS　BRITISH IN
STE
BY RICHARD

R.JACK 1924

NDUSTRIES

EL

JACK, R.A.

LONDON MIDLAND & SCOTTISH RAILWAY COMPANY

LMS   BRITISH I

C

BY G. C

NDUSTRIES
OAL
AUSEN, R.A.

TILBURY FOR

LMS

S.S. "Picard" leaving T

By NORMA

The nightly Tilbury-Dunkerque Service
affords connections with all parts
of the Continent and is the most

THE CONTINENT

bury Marine for Dunkerque

WILKINSON, R.I.

convenient Route from the Midlands
and North of England to Paris,
Basle, Italy, and Central Europe.

vicious retaliatory measures taken by the LMS and the other railway companies to workers who had taken part in the General Strike in 1926. A similarly Orwellian approach was taken by George Clausen in the LMS 'British Industries' series of posters. In 'Coal', for instance, cloth-capped and mufflered miners trek homewards into the setting sun, whilst behind them the winding gear and other pithead equipment stand in sharp relief against the evening sky. Radically different as this intrinsically socialist message was to the conventional middle-class approach of the railway poster, it was also an important historical image to make (even allowing for the cloth cap figure) for the General Strike showed just how ignorant and unsympathetic the middle class were towards the working man and these pictures lent him a recognisable dignity.

As well as social realism, there was an element of economic realism in the 'British Industries' series. The fundamental role of the railways in productive economic activity, by supplying industry with raw materials and distributing its products was, until these posters, ignored by the publicists in favour of such non-productive functions as ferrying people to holiday resorts and leisure activities. Another Royal Academician, Richard Jack, portrayed 'Steel' in this series by emphasising the railway sidings outside some great Clydeside steelworks. Blast furnaces light up the sky, recalling the classics of industrial art – de Loutherbourg's 'Coalbrookdale by Night', Richard Crawshay's 'Nant-y-glo Ironworks', Francis Nicholson's 'Explosion and Fire at Shiffnal', Thomas Allom's 'Lymington Iron Works' – and especially Dickens's description in *The Old Curiosity Shop* of an iron foundry at night 'when the smoke changed to fire, when every chimney spirted up its flame; and places, that had been dark vaults all day, now shone red-hot, with figures moving to and fro within their blazing jaws, and calling to one another with hoarse cries.'

One might argue that such advertising was art for art's sake; that the efforts of the Bauhaus and others in the integration of text and picture had been ignored and that such posters were little more than pictures on the wall. Whilst there is some substance in this hard-line approach, it is also fair to say that the LMS posters, though in an extremely formal way, did bring good contemporary art out of the galleries and into the public eye, where, no doubt, it brought considerable pleasure to waiting travellers. What they did in terms of selling tickets is another matter.

The London and North Eastern Railway's advertising manager, W. M. Teasdale, was also acutely conscious of the necessity for a high pictorial quality of poster work, but he chose the avant-garde rather than the academic approach. He selected artists like Austin Cooper, Tom Purvis, Fred Taylor, A. R. Thompson and Frank Newbould for commissions; some of these were paid retainers by the LNER Frank Brangwyn's 'Royal Border Bridge' was a good example of their early publicity, and around 1925 the LNER furthered their design co-ordination by adapting Eric Gill's famous *sans serif* typeface (derived from Edward Johnston's equally distinguished 'underground letter' of a decade earlier) as standard. Frank Newbould's 'Silver Jubilee' poster of 1935 was one of their best; this new express, strikingly liveried in silver and grey and hauled by streamlined locomotives specially designed by Sir Nigel Gresley – the famous A4 Pacifics, given appropriate names like *Silver Link*, *Silver King*, *Silver Fox* and *Quicksilver* – ushered in the streamline era on Britain's railways. The train was the last word in comfort, luxury and speed and Newbould's progressive design did full justice to the finesse of the LNER's flyer; there was also a handsome commemorative booklet with a similar design in blue and silver on the cover.

119

"LOCOMOTION" driven by George Stephenson

Newbould also produced designs for an 'East Coast Types' series, one of which, 'The Deck-chair Man', is illustrated. Like Stanhope Forbes's track-laying gang poster for the LMS, this captured the quiet dignity of ordinary folk going about their everyday business. The outlines (presumably based on a photograph) and colouring were simple: a blue jersey and hat and the bold red stripes of the deck-chairs were set against a beige and sepia background. Austin Cooper did a fine poster for the perennially popular resort of Scarborough, as well as more prosaic advertisements for track maintenance ('Costs £5,700,000 – Going On All The Time') and the LNER's car-transporting service, which featured an exceedingly Laurel-and-Hardy-type banger, which whilst not the classic Model T was at least a Bull-nose Morris or something similar.

114 Maurice Greiffenhargen's 'Carlisle' heralded a blitz of 'Gateway to . . . ' travel posters in later years. *British Transport Museum (B Sharpe)*

115 'The Permanent Way' by Stanhope Forbes, one of the later series. Contemporary newspapers were frequently moved to comment on the excellence of these LMS posters. *British Transport Museum (B Sharpe)*

116 'Steel' by Richard Jack. Railway advertising normally preferred to divert the eye from such aspects of their activities. Other posters in this series included 'Cotton' by Cayley Robinson and 'The Staffordshire Potteries' by Augustus John. *British Transport Museum (B Sharpe)*

East Coast
Types

No.5 The Deck-chair Man

Travel cheaply by L·N·E·R

Published by the London & North Eastern Railway   *Printed in England*   *Charley & Pickersgill Ltd Lithographers Leeds*

117 'Coal' by Gilbert Clausen, from the 'British Industries' series. The line of loaded coal trucks emphasised the important role which freight played in the railway's economy.
British Transport Museum (B Sharpe)

118 The idea of commissioning paintings from Academicians was first suggested by Norman Wilkinson, who had earlier produced paintings for use in advertisements for the London and North Western Railway's steamer services. To the LMS series he contributed this fine view of the SS *Picard* leaving Tilbury on the Dunkerque service.
British Transport Museum (B Sharpe)

119 London and North Eastern Railway design by Fred Taylor commemorating the 100th anniversary of the Stockton and Darlington Railway.
British Transport Museum (B Sharpe)

120 One of the 'East Coast Types' series by Frank Newbould issued by the LNER to promote the holiday areas the company had taken over from the North Eastern and Great Eastern Railways after the grouping in 1923.
British Transport Museum (B Sharpe)

121

121 1932 poster by AR Thompson offering an interesting visual interpretation of the LNER's cheap fare facilities.
British Transport Museum (B Sharpe)

122 Gay young thingery, London and North Eastern style.
British Transport Museum (B Sharpe)

out at it – in the nicest possible way, even apologising to the Southern for doing so – in a brilliant cubist satire by A. P. Thompson. In the LNER burlesque a sun-hatted, white-socked cherub is dwarfed by enormous, twenty-foot high driving wheels, while the driver tries to speak to him from the dizzy heights of his cab by means of a megaphone. The actual design of the poster was avant-garde in the extreme, stressing the enormous gulf in aesthetic quality that existed between the LNER's publicity and that of its less aesthetically minded rivals. The Southern took the hint (though they did not withdraw the offending poster, continuing to use it with a variety of captions for a good many years) and increased the artistic content of their later posters substantially. When they introduced the 'Devon Belle' Pullman car train they had Severin design their poster, issued jointly with the Pullman Car Company, since the latter remained an independent leaser of its vehicles to railway companies for many years and kept a careful eye on its public image. The speeding observation car at the rear of the train made a good subject, carefully set off against a curiously surreal landscape. There was an excellent 'Summer in the South' series in the late 1930s using 'name' artists and at the end of World War II, shortly before the Southern lost its identity in the 1948 nationalisation of Britain's railways, Leslie Carr gave them a fine study of one of Bulleid's 'West Country' Pacifics at speed for use on posters.

Despite the zeal which W. H. Fraser brought to the line when he was appointed publicity agent in 1924, the Great Western Railway was always something of an also-ran when it came to poster design. Paddington's energies were concentrated on producing an impressive series of glossy illustrated brochures, holiday guides and other promotional material, and poster work was farmed out to printers

TAKE YOUR CAR
BY
L·N·E·R

STILL FURTHER
REDUCED RATES
OUTWARD
3d PER MILE
RETURN
1½d PER MILE

Ask for particulars at L·N·E·R
Stations and Offices

LONDON & NORTH EASTERN RAILWAY

123

One of the most amusing (and at the same time impressively designed) LNER posters was at the expense of the Southern Railway, a rather dull company which was interested in packing commuters into electric trains and little else. They did have a nice line in holiday traffic to the south coast, though, and their favoured medium for this was for many years the famous poster (based on a photograph by Charles E. Brown) of a small boy talking to the driver of the holiday express at the end of the platform at Waterloo. It was a very popular poster with the travelling public, but, in view of the fine stuff being put out by the LMS and the LNER it was, to say the least, a little twee. The LNER hit

123 To compete with road traffic, the LNER offered car-carrying services between London and Scotland. Unlike the position in the early days of transporting horse-drawn carriages by rail, passengers were not allowed to remain in their vehicles. The poster is by Austin Cooper.
British Transport Museum (B Sharpe)

124 When it first appeared in 1935, the LNER's 'Silver Jubilee' express was the last word in comfort, speed and luxury. This poster by Frank Newbould captures the striking outlines of the streamlined locomotives used on the train.
British Transport Museum (B Sharpe)

125 Austin Cooper's 1932 poster for the Yorkshire coast resort of Scarborough.
British Transport Museum (B Sharpe)

126 Thompson's brilliant satire of the Southern Railway's most famous poster.
British Transport Museum (B Sharpe)

127 The butt of Thompson's joke. This poster was reissued many times with different lettering.
British Transport Museum (B Sharpe)

"THE SILVER JUBILEE"

BRITAIN'S FIRST STREAMLINE TRAIN

NEWCASTLE AND LONDON IN 4 HOURS

AVERAGE THROUGHOUT SPEED 67.08 M.P.H.

Weekdays (Saturdays excepted) from 30th. September 1935

NEWCASTLE	dep 10. 0 am	KING'S CROSS	dep 5. 30 pm
DARLINGTON	" 10.42	DARLINGTON	arr. 8. 48
KING'S CROSS	arr. 2. 0 pm	NEWCASTLE	" 9. 30

Connecting trains serve Tyneside and Tees-side

SUPPLEMENTARY FARES: (FOR EACH SINGLE JOURNEY) First Class 5/- Third Class 3/-

LONDON & NORTH EASTERN RAILWAY

LONDON & NORTH EASTERN RAILWAY

124

FRANK NEWBOULD

PRINTED IN GREAT BRITAIN   THE BAYNARD PRESS

SCARBO

1932 BOOKLET FREE FROM T
L·N·E·R INQUIRY C

OROUGH

OWN CLERK, TOWN HALL OR ANY
OFFICE OR AGENCY

PUBLISHED BY THE LONDON AND NORTH EASTERN RAILWAY

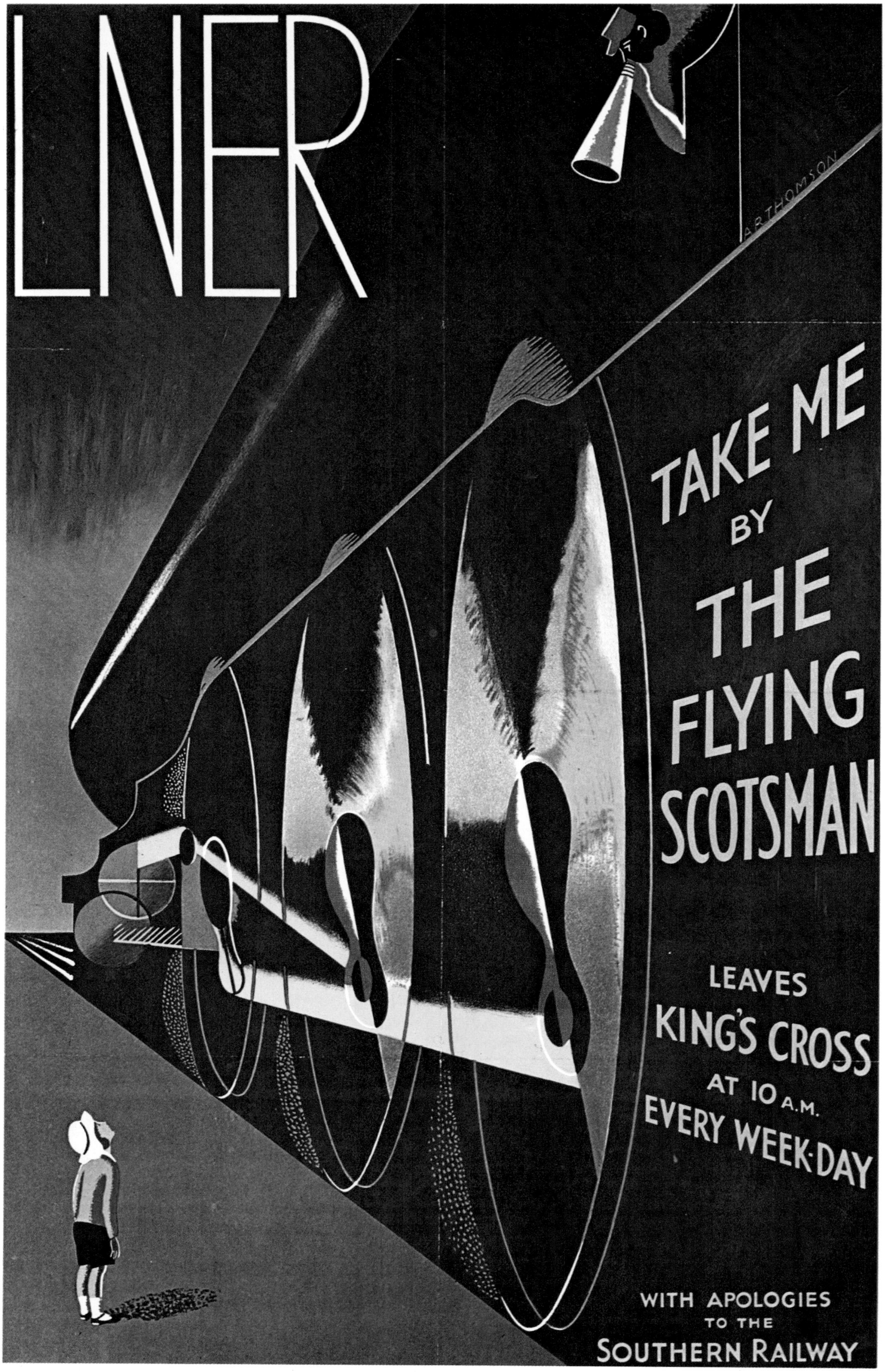
LNER
TAKE ME
BY
THE
FLYING
SCOTSMAN
LEAVES
KING'S CROSS
AT 10 A.M.
EVERY WEEK-DAY
WITH APOLOGIES
TO THE
SOUTHERN RAILWAY
A.R. THOMSON

IM TAKING AN
EARLY HOLIDAY COS
I KNOW SUMMER
COMES SOONEST IN THE SOUTH

SOUTHERN RAILWAY

SOUTHERN RAILWAY ADVERTISING   Ad 3251   JOHNSON RIDDLE & CO. LTD. LONDON S.E.1.

and NOW
200
RESTAURANT CARS
ON
L·N·E·R TRAINS
LONDON AND NORTH EASTERN RAILWAY

to design. This obsolete practice, dating from the bad old days of the letterpress posters, was not finally abandoned by the GWR until the early 1930s. Consequently the early days of the reconstituted GWR saw a lot of real lead zeppelins on the hoardings, although in 1924 they issued quite a pleasing, if somewhat naive poster for the two-hour Birmingham expresses (their flagwaver) in which a natty gent in spats and a bowler held a stopwatch in one hand and pumped the driver's hand with the other, saying 'Splendid run! Thank you!' In later years they heeded the highly professional approach to poster work which had been adopted by the LMS and LNER and commissioned posters by recognised artists, though here again they fell victim to poor planning, on two counts. Firstly, by using, by and large, people like Frank Newbould, Fred Taylor and

128 A contrast in the train accommodation of 1830 and 1930 by AR Thompson.
British Transport Museum (B Sharpe)

McKnight Kauffer, their posters lacked individuality and a specifically GWR flavour, since these artists tended to be already identified with other companies. Secondly, there was a pronounced bias in favour of representational art, which tended to muzzle someone like McKnight Kauffer and makes one wonder why the GWR employed him in the first place. Frank Pick had established very early in his career that stunning results were more likely to be achieved if the artist was given a free hand but even when the co-operation of a local authority was not involved the GWR liked to lay down hard and

110

fast rules for its artists. An exhibition of McKnight Kauffer's work at the American Museum in Bath in 1975 showed very clearly that the 'Devon' posters commissioned from him by the GWR in the late 1930s, were tame and restricted when exhibited alongside the American Airlines posters produced when he returned to the States shortly afterwards. The Newbould/Taylor school of landscape art was what the GWR directors liked and, although the railway preferred to append the name of the managing director to its posters rather than identify the artist, the two examples of original artwork illustrated in this chapter clearly belong to the landscape school and no doubt fulfilled their purpose.

On the continent inventiveness in railway poster design seemed to know no bounds, though the subjects covered were by and large similar to those deemed effective in Britain – prestige expresses, holiday traffic and the like. Whereas the LNER posterists like Newbould and Cooper opted for a softer, pastel-coloured approach, the French went in for a much harder outline achieved through the bold use of fractured colour planes. Cubism, the Bauhaus and montage techniques were the principal influences; Roger Broders' 'Sainte-Maxime' poster of the mid 1920s for the PLM featured a striking pattern of red sails and blue water, seen through the silhouetted forms of palm trees. It makes little attempt at a realistic representation of the resort, but fuses essential elements – sea, palms, the sweep of the coastline – into an image of opulence and exoticism. Majorelle's Beardsleyesque design for the PLM's 'Le Maroc par Marseille' (elements of cubism can also be seen in the figure, set off so effectively against the foreign landscape) was another good example of image-mongering. The commodity had to be made attractive, and yet at the same time it had to relate to the potential market's own preconceived notions.

So Majorelle's figure, appealingly mysterious, appears against a reassuringly normal-looking landscape calculated not to put too strong a fear of the alien into the potential traveller.

The formal symmetry of this design stands in stark contrast to some of the Bauhaus-influenced work of Roger Broders. Instead of cramming detail into every square inch of the poster, Broders experimented with the use of large areas of blank colour. In his 'Marseille – Point de Départ de la Côte d'Azur' he used a considerable area of neutral blue to emphasise the dynamics of montage in the design. The rakish angle of the lines of type combined with the orthodox perspective of the train and motor coach to give a remarkable impression of movement towards a fixed destination. The concept of movement in an abstract sense, as opposed to what one did to divert oneself on the journey, by patronising the dining-car for instance, was of special interest to Broders and it was one which was of particular relevance to the travel poster. Thus his poster for Mont Blanc (reached by PLM motor coaches) had the lettering as a spiralling path, down which the coach travelled to reach the very desirable mountain in the background.

129 One of the Southern Railway's better posters, designed by Raymond Savignac. Observation cars like this were frequently used to bring up the rear of trains in the streamline era of the 1930s.
British Transport Museum (B Sharpe)

The **DEVON BELLE**

Fridays, Saturdays, Sundays and Mondays in each direction

dep	12.0 noon	Waterloo	arr	5.20 pm
arr	3.16 pm	Sidmouth Jct.	dep	2.3 pm
arr	3.36 pm	Exeter Ctl.	dep	1.40 pm
arr	5.32 pm	Ilfracombe	dep	12.0 noon
arr	5.36 pm	Plymouth Friary	dep	11.30 am

NEW!

ALL-PULLMAN TRAIN TO THE WEST OF ENGLAND
with Observation Car
SOUTHERN RAILWAY & PULLMAN CAR COMPANY

MINEHEAD
THE GATEWAY TO EXMOOR
REACHED BY GREAT WESTERN RAILWAY

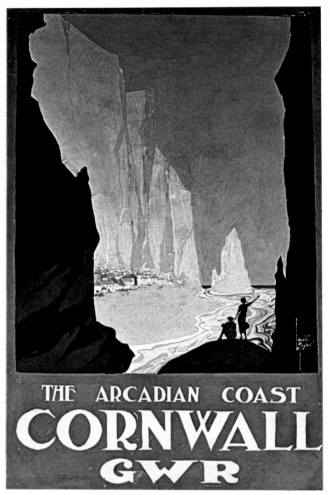

THE ARCADIAN COAST
CORNWALL
GWR

130, 131 Two examples of the Great Western Railway's output in the 1930s, when they began to employ recognised artists rather than rely on homespun talent.
Great Western Railway Museum, Swindon (Ian Krause)

132 Pierre Fixmasseau seemed particularly adept at putting the speed and power of locomotives to good effect in his graphic designs. This 1929 poster for the luxury Côte d'Azur Pullman trains of the PLM adopts a track-level viewpoint to emphasise the streamlined 'windcutter' profile of the train engine.
La Vie du Rail

133 Poster by Théodoro for the Paris-Orléans Railway stressing the close co-operation between rail, sea and air services in the profitable Morocco traffic.
La Vie du Rail

134 Another high-quality poster for the Côte d'Azur trains, designed by Emile-André Schefer for the PLM. The careful detailing stresses the bulk of the locomotive against a simpler and more muted background. In this splendid poster, the elegance of the typography contrasts strongly with the more severe sans serif styles used in Britain at the same time.
La Vie du Rail

135 An example of the high standard of PLM advertising art in the late 1920s and early 1930s. It is signed J Majorelle.
La Vie du Rail

136 The PLM company was not afraid to experiment with bold outlines and strong colour. This Saint-Maxime poster of *circa* 1930 is the work of Roger Broders.
La Vie du Rail

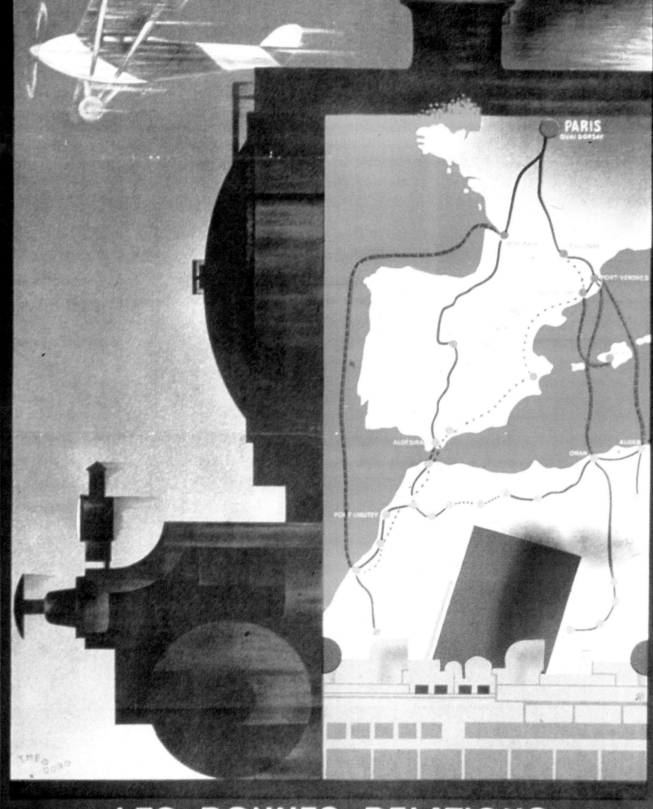

PARIS-LYON-MÉDITERRANÉE

Emile André
SCHEFER

LA CÔTE D'AZUR
A UNE NUIT DE PARIS
.trains de luxe.
.trains rapides.
1ères et 2èmes classes

ROGER
BRODERS

MARSEILLE
POINT DE DÉPART
DE LA
COTE D'AZUR

137

One of the most advanced of the continental posterists of this period was Adolphe Jean-Marie Mouron, who signed his work 'Cassandre'. His products found their way to many countries, notably his exquisite 'Venezia' with the symmetrically reflected silhouette of a Venetian gondolier, the 'Wagon Lit' poster of 1930 and the 'Etoile du Nord' of 1927. In the last-named, the element of the railway is reduced to a starkly simple pattern of gleaming lines leading the eye up to a bright star on the horizon. Traces of this classic poster may be found in British Rail's 1975 'Sleep a Night and Gain a Day' poster, which modifies the original design little, except for substituting the front end of a diesel locomotive for the star and being coloured in tones of turquoise against Cassandre's blue. In the mid 1930s he also did work for the London, Midland and Scottish Railway in Britain, one of the few instances of an established foreign artist (he was born in the Ukraine of French parents) contributing posters to a British company.

As has been remarked earlier, it was not common in the pre-World War I era for the actual train to appear in the poster. In the 1920s and 30s, though, an increasing number of designers began to see the train as the very symbol of movement and power. This was frequently balanced by the juxtaposition of other forms of transport: the powerful automobile in Pierre Fixmasseau's poster for the Nord company's connecting bus and train services, the aeroplane and ship in Theodoro's 'France – Algérie – Maroc: Les Bonnes Relations' for the Chemins der Fer de Paris à Orléans. Their presence is understandable, for these alternative forms of transport were already beginning to provide serious competition to the monopoly which the railways had held

for so long and it was essential for the latter to be seen as holding an inter-acting stake in other operations.

The inter-war period was also the heyday of the great expresses, the 'Flying Scotsman' and 'Silver Jubilee' in Britain, the 'Twentieth Century Limited' and the 'Empire State Express' in the States, the 'Blue Train' and the 'Flêche d'Or' in France. The emphasis had to change, then, from the places the train served to the train itself; prestige, speed and luxury were the passwords. Thus Fixmasseau's 1929 poster for the Pullman expresses to the Côte d'Azur adapted a low angle, track level view of the approaching express, with the Riviera scenery playing a very subsidiary role in the background. The engine has been smoothed in outline and made bullet-like at the front end (prototype locomotives frequently had wind-cutter noses which were of doubtful value in

137-138 Further examples of Broders' work for the PLM. Note the strong sense of motion in both designs and the implication that, by train or by road, the PLM will get you there.
La Vie du Rail

139 Cassandre's famous 'Etoile du Nord' poster of 1927.
CJ McBarr collection (HP Grain)

140 A classic Italian State Railways design by Cassandre. The delicate lighting and rhythms of this poster suit the subject admirably.
La Vie du Rail

141 This design by Pierre Fixmasseau issued on behalf of the Nord and STARN organisations hints of German influence in the strong and forceful outlines of the locomotive and motor car.
La Vie du Rail

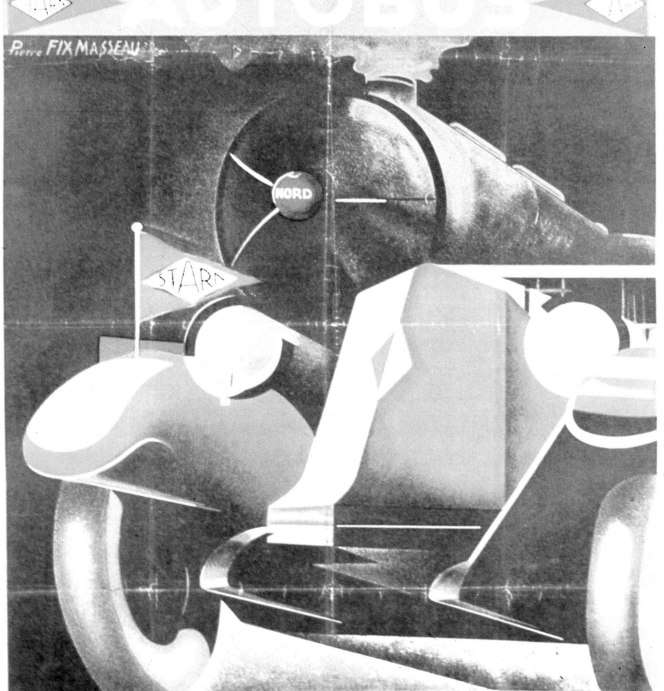

142 Undoubtedly the star turn of the Côte d'Azur prestige expresses was the 'Blue Train', operated jointly by the Nord, PLM and Wagons-Lits companies. The aerial view-point, emphasising the train's exhaust, combines well with the adventurous style of lettering.
La Vie du Rail

143 The full splendour of luxury travel in the 1930s comes out in this joint Nord-Wagons Lits-PLM design. The symmetrical perspective and picking out and highlighting of details of the interior fittings set up a virtual three-dimensional effect.
La Vie du Rail

144 An early, immediately pre-war SNCF poster for Soulac, showing how far the design of seaside posters had progressed since the genteel days of the nineteenth century. *La Vie du Rail*

145 An appeal to American railroad men for diligence and efficiency in the war effort.
Union Pacific Railroad Museum collection

NOTICE
TO RAILWAY PASSENGERS

NOTICE IS HEREBY GIVEN

that, due to the National Emergency, the following alterations in Passenger Train travel, as applying to the Railways in Great Britain, will come into force on and from MONDAY, 11th SEPTEMBER, 1939:-

1. Passenger Train Services.
The Passenger Train Services will be considerably curtailed and decelerated. For details see the Company's Notices.

2. Cancellation of Reduced Fare Facilities.
Excursion and Reduced Fare facilities (except Monthly Return, Week-end, and Workmen's tickets) will be discontinued until further notice.

3. Season and Traders' Tickets.
Season and Traders' tickets will continue to be issued.

4. Reservation of Seats, Compartments, Etc.
The reservation of seats and compartments, and saloons for private parties will be discontinued.

5. Restaurant Cars and Sleeping Cars.
Restaurant Car facilities will be withdrawn, and only a very limited number of Sleeping Cars will be available.

By Order
11th September, 1939. THE RAILWAY EXECUTIVE COMMITTEE.

ground, the table, seats and girl's legs stand in a remarkably three-dimensional relief. All is harmonious, exclusive, unruffled.

As with the effect of the Great War on the art nouveau and Hassall schools of posterists, the coming of world war in 1939 marked the end of an era of poster design. Of the wartime railway posters themselves, suffice it to say that the fervour and belligerence which we have seen in the Great War gave way to more pragmatic exhortations, towards increased production, towards economy ('Is Your Journey Really Necessary?') and towards vigilance (Billy Brown of London Town, who directed Londoners' attention to the infidel Hun in the same Underground carriage). Even the flag-waving 'In War and Peace We Serve' poster put out by Britain's big four companies might be taken as stressing the values of painstaking co-operation in running trains for long distances over once-rival lines, as well as overt patriotism.

And after the war? This is really where the golden age of railway posters came to an end, when the cheapness and flexibility of photographically based artwork took over from the skill and ingenuity of the purely graphic designer. Speaking of advertisements for proprietary products in his book *Posters*, Bevis Hillier has called this 'a surrender to that old cunning aim of the manufacturer, which the early pictorial posterists had only with difficulty managed to frustrate, to have his product illustrated . . . with complete faithfulness.' Out went the speeding expresses, bathing belles and jolly fishermen; in came endless crystal-clear pretty pictures of the Pyrenees or the Rhine Valley, which did nothing to improve upon the imaginative interpretations of graphic artists like Broders or Taylor a quarter-century earlier. In the past twenty-five years or so there have been exceptions: notably the SNCF's bold move in commissioning Utrillo and Dali to design posters, or the sympathetic understanding of the place of the train in the landscape in the work of John Goss and his colleagues at the British Rail Photographic Unit. Late in 1975 London Transport issued a McKnight Kauffer poster for the Natural History Museum, originally designed in 1939, and the sheer class and style of this poster put much other work to shame. Class was what the great age of poster design set out to give the railway, its trains and the places it served. We are the poorer without it.

146 An austerely functional poster put out by the Railway Executive in Britain at the outbreak of World War II. Contingency plans had in fact been drawn up for the evacuation of civilians and a drastic curtailment of services some months before war was actually declared.
Imperial War Museum

147 Poster issued on behalf of all four British main-line railway companies to emphasise the high degree of co-operative effort involved in running trains in wartime.
British Transport Museum (B Sharpe)

148 One of the last flowerings of the great age of railway graphic art before the rapid influx of photo-based advertising after the war. This Southern Railway poster of *circa* 1946 was the work of Leslie Carr; this example was printed without wording, which could be added as required later.
British Transport Museum (B Sharpe)

decreasing wind resistance, but which certainly added a prestigiously sleek look). Since French engines frequently carried a labyrinth of piping around the outside of the boiler, this unsightly clutter has been removed and the only evidence of the 'works' is the blur of wheels and connecting-rods. The sweeping patterns of track and exhaust were used to good effect in the joint Nord-Wagons Lits-PLM poster of 1923 for the then newly introduced 'Blue Train'. Again, the train itself was felt to have sufficient image for it to dominate completely the balancing yachts on the azure sea.

A poster by Emile-André Schefer for the PLM's Côte d'Azur 'trains de luxe' and 'trains rapides' showed that the moment of maximum power when the engine first sets its train in motion could be equally as effective as high-speed running as a subject for design. Set off against a modernistic art deco typeface, his big express engine seems full of life, emphasised by the careful attention to detail and the proud plume of smoke. The plush interiors of these trains also offered considerable scope for imaginative poster design and few works conveyed the elegance and luxury of travel in the inter-war years so effectively as the joint Nord-Wagons Lits-PLM 'Londres-Vichy Pullman' advertisement. The two passengers, right down to the girl's cloche hat and her escort's double-breasted suit and spats, are the epitome of the svelte bourgeoisie which the train hoped to cater for. Against the rich blue